interchange

English for international communication
Jack C. Richards

INTRO

Student's Book

CAMBRIDGE
UNIVERSITY PRESS

PUBLISHED BY THE PRESS SYNDICATE OF THE UNIVERSITY OF CAMBRIDGE
The Pitt Building, Trumpington Street, Cambridge, United Kingdom

CAMBRIDGE UNIVERSITY PRESS
The Edinburgh Building, Cambridge CB2 2RU, UK   http://www.cup.cam.ac.uk
40 West 20th Street, New York, NY 10011–4211, USA   http://www.cup.org
10 Stamford Road, Oakleigh, Melbourne 3166, Australia

First published 1994
Fifteenth printing 1999

Printed in the United Kingdom at the University Press, Cambridge

Typeset in Century Schoolbook

Library of Congress Cataloging-in-Publication Data

Richards, Jack C.
Interchange: English for international communication: intro
student's book/Jack C. Richards.
p. cm.
ISBN 0-521-46744-6
1. English language – Textbooks for foreign speakers.
2. Communication, International – Problems, exercises, etc.
I. Title. II. Title: Intro student's book.
PE1128.R456   1994
428.2'4 – dc20   91-17933
                                                                 CIP

ISBN 0 521 46744 6   Intro Student's Book
ISBN 0 521 46742 X   Intro Teacher's Manual
ISBN 0 521 46743 8   Intro Workbook
ISBN 0 521 46741 1   Intro Class Cassettes
ISBN 0 521 55608 2   Intro Lab Guide
ISBN 0 521 55613 9   Intro Lab Cassette Set

Split editions:
ISBN 0 521 47185 0   Intro Student's Book A
ISBN 0 521 47186 9   Intro Student's Book B
ISBN 0 521 47187 7   Intro Workbook A
ISBN 0 521 47188 5   Intro Workbook B
ISBN 0 521 46740 3   Intro Student Cassette A
ISBN 0 521 47189 3   Intro Student Cassette B

Book design: Peter Ducker
Layout and design services: Adventure House, McNally Graphic Design
Cover design: Tom Wharton

Contents

Plan of Intro Book

	Topics	Functions	Grammar
UNIT 1	**Topics** Alphabet; greetings and leave-takings; titles of address; classroom objects; telephone numbers	**Functions** Introducing yourself; spelling names and words; saying phone numbers; giving classroom instructions	**Grammar** Possessive adjectives *my, your, his,* and *her;* the verb *be:* affirmative statements and contractions; numbers 1–10; articles *a* and *an;* imperatives (affirmative)
UNIT 2	**Topics** Personal items, possessions, and locations in a room	**Functions** Naming objects; finding the owner of an item; asking for and giving location	**Grammar** Plurals; *this* and *these;* possessive of names; possessive adjectives; the verb *be:* yes/no questions and short answers with *it* and *they;* prepositions of place
UNIT 3	**Topics** Countries; regions; nationalities; languages	**Functions** Asking for and giving information about country of origin, nationality, native language, and geographical locations	**Grammar** Affirmative and negative statements with *be;* adjectives of nationality; questions and short answers with *be*
UNIT 4	**Topics** Clothing, colors; weather, temperatures, and seasons of the year	**Functions** Asking about and describing clothing; talking about current activities; talking about the weather	**Grammar** Present continuous: affirmative and negative statements; numbers to 100; adjectives after *be*

Review of Units 1–4

	Topics	Functions	Grammar
UNIT 5	**Topics** Times of the day, clock time; daily activities; Saturday chores	**Functions** Asking for and telling time; asking about and describing current activities	**Grammar** Present continuous: *what + doing,* yes/no questions and short answers; Wh-questions; adverbs of time
UNIT 6	**Topics** Transportation; family relationships; daily habits; days of the week	**Functions** Asking for and giving information about where you live, how you go to work, and what you do every day	**Grammar** Present tense: affirmative and negative statements; third-person singular endings; irregular verbs and yes/no and Wh-questions; present time expressions
UNIT 7	**Topics** Homes; rooms; furniture	**Functions** Asking about and describing different homes; saying what furniture is in a room	**Grammar** Present tense: yes/no questions and short answers; *There's /There are* and *There's no/There aren't any*
UNIT 8	**Topics** Occupations; places of work; salaries	**Functions** Asking and giving information about what people do, where they work, and how they like their jobs	**Grammar** Present tense: Wh-questions with *do;* descriptive adjectives; placement of adjectives before nouns

Review of Units 5–8

Introduction

Interchange is a multi-level course in English as a second or foreign language for young adults and adults. The course covers the skills of listening, speaking, reading, and writing, with particular emphasis on listening and speaking. The primary goal of the course is to teach communicative competence – that is, the ability to communicate in English according to the situation, purpose, and roles of the participants. *Interchange* reflects the fact that English is the world's major language of international communication and is not limited to any one country, region, or culture. The *Intro* level is designed for beginning students needing a thorough presentation of basic functions, grammar, and vocabulary. It prepares students to enter Level 1 of the course.

COURSE LENGTH

Interchange is a self-contained course covering all four language skills. Each level covers between 60 and 90 hours of class instruction time. Depending on how the book is used, however, more or less time may be utilized. The Teacher's Manual gives detailed suggestions for optional activities to extend each unit. Where less time is available, a level can be taught in approximately 60 hours by reducing the amount of time spent on Interchange Activities, reading, writing, optional activities, and the Workbook.

COURSE COMPONENTS OF INTRO

Student's Book The Student's Book contains sixteen units, with a review unit after every four units. There are four review units in all. Following Unit 16 is a set of communicative activities called Interchange Activities, one for each unit of the book. Word lists at the end of the Student's Book contain key vocabulary and expressions used in each unit. The Student's Book is available in split edition, A and B, each containing 8 units.

Teacher's Manual A separate Teacher's Manual contains detailed suggestions on how to teach the course, lesson-by-lesson notes, an extensive set of follow-up activities, complete answer keys to the Student's Book and Workbook exercises, four tests for use in class, test answer keys, and transcripts of those listening activities not printed in the Student's Book or in the tests. The tests can be photocopied

and distributed to students after each review unit is completed.

Workbook The Workbook contains stimulating and varied exercises that provide additional practice on the teaching points presented in the Student's Book. A variety of exercise types is used to develop students' skills in grammar, reading, writing, spelling, vocabulary, and pronunciation. The Workbook can be used both for classwork and for homework. The Workbook is available in split editions.

Class Cassettes A set of cassettes for class use accompanies the Student's Book. The cassettes contain recordings of the word power activities, conversations, grammar focus summaries, pronunciation exercises, listening activities, and readings, as well as recordings of the listening exercises used in the tests. A variety of native-speaker voices and accents is used, along with some non-native speakers of English. Exercises that are recorded on the cassettes are indicated with the symbol 🔳.

Student Cassettes Two cassettes are available for students to use for self-study. The Student Cassettes contain selected recordings of conversations, grammar, and pronunciation exercises from the Student's Book. Student Cassette A corresponds to Units 1–8 and Student Cassette B to Units 9–16.

APPROACH AND METHODOLOGY

Interchange teaches students to use English for everyday situations and purposes related to work, school, social life, and leisure. The underlying philosophy of the course is that learning a second language is more rewarding, meaningful, and effective when the language is used for authentic communication. Information-sharing activities provide a maximum amount of student-generated communication. Throughout *Interchange*, students have the opportunity to personalize the language they learn and make use of their own life experiences and world knowledge.

The course has the following key features:

Integrated Syllabus *Interchange* has an integrated, multi-skills syllabus that links grammar and communicative functions. The course recognizes grammar as an essential component of second language proficiency. However, it presents grammar communicatively, with controlled accuracy-based activities leading to fluency-based communicative practice. The syllabus also contains the four skills of listening, speaking, reading, and writing, as well as pronunciation and vocabulary.

Adult and International Content   *Interchange* deals with contemporary topics that are of high interest and relevance to both students and teachers. Each unit includes real-world information on a variety of topics.

Enjoyable and Useful Learning Activities
A wide variety of interesting and enjoyable activities forms the basis for each unit. The course makes extensive use of pair work, small group activities, role plays, and information-sharing activities. Practice exercises allow for a maximum amount of individual student practice and enable learners to personalize and apply the language they learn. Throughout the course, natural and useful language is presented that can be used in real-life situations.

WHAT EACH UNIT OF INTRO CONTAINS

Each unit in *Interchange* contains the following kinds of exercises:

Snapshot   The Snapshots provide interesting information about the world, introduce the topic of the unit and develop vocabulary. The teacher can either present these exercises in class as reading or discussion activities, or have students read them by themselves in class or for homework, using their dictionaries if necessary.

Conversation   The Conversations introduce the new grammar of each unit in a communicative context and present functions and conversational expressions. The teacher can either present the Conversations with the Class Cassettes or read the dialogs aloud.

Pronunciation   These exercises focus on important features of spoken English, including stress, rhythm, intonation, reductions, and sound contrasts.

Grammar Focus   The new grammar of each unit is presented in color panels and is followed by practice activities that move from controlled to freer practice. These activities always give students a chance to use the grammar they have learned for real communication.

Listening   The listening activities develop a wide variety of listening skills, including listening for gist, listening for details, and inferring meaning from

context. These exercises often require completing an authentic task while listening, such as taking telephone messages. The recordings offer natural conversational English with the pauses, hesitations, and interruptions that occur in real speech.

Word Power   The Word Power activities develop students' vocabulary through a variety of interesting tasks, such as word maps. Most of these are recorded.

Writing   The writing exercises include practical writing tasks that extend and reinforce the teaching points in the unit and introduce students to composition skills. The Teacher's Manual shows how to use these exercises to focus on the process of writing.

Reading   Beginning in Unit 5, there are reading passages designed to develop a variety of reading skills, including guessing words from context, skimming, scanning, and making inferences. Various text types adapted from authentic sources are included.

Interchange Activities   The Interchange Activities are pair work and group work tasks involving information sharing and role playing to encourage real communication. These exercises are a central part of the course and allow students to extend and personalize what they have learned in each unit.

1 Hello. My name is Jennifer Wan.

1 SNAPSHOT

снёпшот
[snæpʃt] моментальный снимок (§ ниц)
[fə:st] имя

POPULAR FIRST NAMES IN THE U.S.A.

Females [fiːmel] Males [maɪl]

Females		Males	
Jennifer	Sarah	Michael	John
Nicole	Deborah	Robert	Brian
Lisa	Mary	David	William
Michelle	Katherine	James	Steven
Linda	Jessica	Christopher	Matthew

полный
[kəmpliːt] [infəmeʃn]
Complete the information. сообщение
[feɪvərit]
My favorite girl's name in English: _Jennifer_
My favorite boy's name in English: _Robert_
A popular first name in my country: _Haim_
[kʌntri] [maɪ]

2 CONVERSATION 🔲

[kɔnvəseiʃn] разговор (диалог)

Listen and practice.

Jennifer: Hello. My name is Jennifer Wan.
Michael: Hi. I'm Michael Lynch.
Jennifer: Nice to meet you, Michael.
Michael: Nice to meet you, too, Jennifer.
I'm sorry, what's your last name?
Is it Wong?
Jennifer: No, *Wan*. W-A-N. And how do you
spell Lynch?
Michael: L-Y-N-C-H.

3 THE ALPHABET 🔲

1 Listen and practice.

A B C D E F G H I J K L M N O P Q R S T U V W X Y Z
a b c d e f g h i j k l m n o p q r s t u v w x y z

[speð)waːk] [aʊt] [faɪnd] [aʊt]
2 *Pair work* Spell your name. Then find out your partner's name
and your teacher's name. Spell their names.
[ðiːts]

4 GRAMMAR FOCUS: *my, your, his, her* 🔊

> My name is Jennifer.
>
> His name is Michael.
>
> Her name is Nicole.

What's **your** name?	**My** name is Jennifer.
What's **his** name?	**His** name is Michael.
What's **her** name?	**Her** name is Nicole.

What's = What is

Group work: "The Name Game"   Make a circle. [ɡɜːl](круг)

Learn the names of your classmates.   [meik] делать

[lɜːn]

A: My name is Juan.

B: His name is Juan. I'm Su Hee.

C: His name is Juan. Her name is Su Hee. I'm Keiko.

5 LISTENING 🔊

listening слушающий   конвэрзэйшнз

1   Who are they? Listen to the conversations. Spell their last names.

a) Whitney ....
(She's a singer.)

b) Jackie ....
(He's a movie star.)

c) Steven ....
(He's a film director.)

2   *Pair work*   Cover the names. Now ask about each person. [kʌvə] [nau][əbaut]

A: What's her (his) name?   [aːsk] [hiːz][pɜːsn]

B: ...

A: How do you spell her (his) name?

B: ...

3

6 CONVERSATION 🔲

Listen and practice.

Victor: Excuse me, are you Jennifer Wan?
Lisa: No, I'm not. She's over there.
Victor: I'm sorry.

Victor: Excuse me, are you Jennifer Wan?
Jennifer: Yes, I am.
Victor: I think this is your book.
Jennifer: You're right. It's my English book.
            Thank you.
Victor: By the way, I'm Victor Garcia.
Jennifer: It's nice to meet you, Victor.

7 GRAMMAR FOCUS: The verb *be* 🔲

I'm Victor Garcia.	**Are you** Jennifer Wan?	**I'm** = I am
You're right.	**No, I'm not.**	**You're** = You are
She's over there. (**Jennifer is** over there.)	**Yes, I am.**	**She's** = She is
He's here. (**Victor is** here.)		**He's** = He is
It's my English book.		**It's** = It is

1 Complete the conversations.

Nicole: Excuse me, _are_ you Steven Carlson?
David: No, _I'm_ not. _He's_ over there. My name _is_ David Bloom.
Nicole: Thanks, David.

Nicole: Are you Steven Carlson?
Steven: Yes, I _am_ .
Nicole: _I'm_ Nicole Johnson.
Steven: _It is_ nice to meet you. I think _you're_ in my math class.
Nicole: Yes, I _am_ . And I think this _is_ your book.
Steven: Yes, _it's_ my math workbook. My name _it's_ here. Thank you!

2 *Class activity*   Write your name on a piece of paper. Put it into a pile.
Choose the name of another student. Find the other student.

A: Excuse me, are you Maria Bravo?   A: Hi. Are you Maria Bravo?
B: No, I'm not.   C: Yes, I am . . .

8 NUMBERS 🔲

1 Listen and practice.

0	1	2	3	4	5	6	7	8	9	10
zero (oh)	one	two	three	four	five	six	seven	eight	nine	ten

2 Say these numbers.

3 *Group work* Make a list of the names and telephone numbers in your group.

A: What's your telephone number?
B: It's 555-2916.

▶ **Interchange 1:
Directory Assistance**

Call Directory Assistance for some telephone numbers. Student A looks at page IC-2 and Student B looks at page IC-4.

9 LISTENING 🔲

Victor is making a list of telephone numbers of students in his class. He's talking to Sarah Smith. Listen and write the numbers.

Name	Telephone number
David Bloom	
Steven Carlson	555-9173
Nicole Johnson	
Lisa Liu	
Michael Lynch	
Brian Noguchi	
Sarah Smith	
Jennifer Wan	555-2947

10 WORD POWER

1 Listen, and complete with **a** or **an**.

[ʃæmplit]
заломити

a) This is ....*a*.... book.

b) This is ....*an*.... English book.

c) This is ....*a*.... notebook.

[i'reizir]

d) This is ...*an*... eraser.

[ʃin] веще

e) This is ...*a*..... dictionary. [dikʃənri]

Словарь

f) This is ...*an*.. umbrella.

гид бреш

2 Find these things in your classroom.

table	map	cassette player
chair	pencil	wastebasket
desk	envelope	English dictionary
board	piece of paper	

A: This is a table.
B: How do you spell *table*?
A: T-A-B-L-E.

---

11 GREETINGS AND TITLES

1 Listen and practice. (**Mr., Mrs., Miss,** and **Ms.** are formal.)

Saying hello

Hi.
Hello.
Good morning.
Good afternoon.
Good evening.

Saying good-bye

Bye.
Bye-bye.
Good-bye. Have a nice day.
See you tomorrow.
Good night.

2 Practice the expressions with your classmates.

12 INSTRUCTIONS 🔊

1 Listen.

a) Close your book, please.

[klouz]

b) Open your notebook.

[oupen]

c) Take out a pencil.

d) Write your name in your
notebook.

[rait]

e) Open your dictionary.

[oupen] dictionary [neybug]

f) Find the word *eraser*.

[faind] [wə:d] [ireiziz]

g) Say the word *eraser*.

сиʔ

h) Please go to the board.

i) Write the word *eraser* on
the board.

2 *Class activity* Listen to your teacher. Follow the instructions.

3 *Pair work* Write six instructions. Read the instructions to your
partner. Then follow your partner's instructions.

2 What's this called in English?

1 SNAPSHOT

THINGS PEOPLE CARRY

an address book

credit cards

a hairbrush

glasses

keys

a comb

pens

a wallet

a driver's license

What are you carrying today? ....

2 SPELLING AND PRONUNCIATION: Plurals 🔲

Listen and practice. Notice the spelling.

s = /s/		s = /z/		s = /ɪz/	
book	books	credit card	credit cards	glass	glasses
wallet	wallets	key	keys	license	licenses
map	maps	pen	pens	hairbrush	hairbrushes

3 CONVERSATION 🔲

Listen and practice.

Kumiko: What's this called in English, Sarah?
Sarah: It's an eyeglass case.
Kumiko: And what are these called? Eyeglasses?
Sarah: Eyeglasses, or just "glasses." And these are sunglasses.
Kumiko: Well, your sunglasses are very . . . nice.
Sarah: Thank you. They're new.

8

4 GRAMMAR FOCUS: *this, these*; singular and plural nouns 🔊

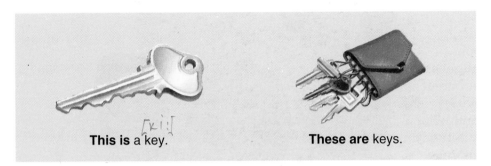

This is a key.

These are keys.

1 What are these things called in English? Write a sentence for each item. Then listen to the sentences and practice them.

handbag   tissues   photos   address book   umbrella
glasses   calculator   newspaper   briefcase

a) This is umbrella .

b) These are glasses .

c) This is calculator

d) This is handbag

e) This is briefcase

f) These are tissues

g) This is newspaper

h) There are photos

i) This is address book

2 *Pair work* Put four things from your pocket, wallet, or bag on the desk. Cover them with a piece of paper. Your partner guesses what they are.

A: I think this is a credit card.
B: No.
A: It's a library card.
B: You're right.

5 CONVERSATION

Listen and practice.

Mrs. Lee: Excuse me, Katherine.
            Is this your umbrella?
Katherine: Let me see. No, it's not.
Mrs. Lee: Maybe it's Alice's umbrella.
Katherine: No, her umbrella is different.
            Oh, I know. I think it's Daniel's.
Mrs. Lee: Daniel, is this your umbrella?
Daniel: Yes, it is. Thank you. Actually,
            it's my daughter's umbrella.

6 GRAMMAR FOCUS: Possessives; yes/no questions with *be*

This is **my** umbrella.
This is **your** book.
This is **our** classroom.
These are **Robert's** keys. These are **his** keys.
These are **Sarah's** glasses. These are **her** glasses.
Mrs. Lee is **Katherine and Daniel's** teacher.
She is **their** teacher. [tiʧer]

Is this Alice's umbrella?
Yes, **it is**.
No, **it's not**.
Are these Daniel's keys?
Yes, **they are**.
No, **they're not**.

Notice the pronunciation of the possessive **'s**:	
Robert's	/s/
Daniel's	/z/
Alice's	/ɪz/

1 Complete the conversations. Then practice them.

A: __Is__ this your calculator?
B: No, it's __not__. __My__ calculator is different.

A: __Are__ these Jennifer's sunglasses?
B: No, __it's__ not. Maybe they're Nicole's.

A: Mr. and Mrs. Lee, __are__ your telephone number 555-1287?
B: No, __our__ number is 555-2287.

A: __Is this__ Lisa's address book?
B: Yes, __it__ is. __She's__ name is right here.

A: __Are__ your keys?
B: Yes, they __my__. Thank you very much.

A: __Are__ your newspaper?
B: Let me see. No, __it's not__. It's Michael's.
__He's__ name and address are here.

2 *Pair work*   Ask your partner a question about each picture.

A: Is this Yung's newspaper?
B: No, it's not his newspaper.

a) Yung

b) Noriko

c) Eric

d) Helen

e) Carmen and Hector

f) Julio

3 *Group work*   Put three things from your wallet, briefcase, or handbag in a box. Find the owner of each item.

A: Is this your pen, Juan?
B: No, it's not. I think it's Su Hee's.

A: Is this your pen, Su Hee?
C: Let me see. Yes, it's my pen.

---

7 LISTENING 📼

Sarah is cleaning up the classroom.
Who owns these things? Listen and check the right name.

	Jennifer	*Michael*	*Nicole*	*Steven*
calculator	....	....	....	....
sunglasses	....	....	....	....
book bag	....	....	....	....
hairbrush	....	....	....	....

8 CONVERSATION

Listen and practice.

Mr. Brown: Thanks for watching the baby tonight. Everything is ready.

Katherine: Thank you, Mr. Brown. By the way, where is the television?

Mr. Brown: It's in this cabinet.

Katherine: And where is the remote control?

Mr. Brown: I don't know. Oh, it's on the sofa, under the cushion.

Katherine: Great. Oh, just one more question. Where is the baby?

Mr. Brown: She's in bed! Her bedroom is right there.

9 PREPOSITIONS OF PLACE

  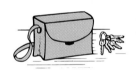  

| in | on | under | next to | behind | in front of |

Complete these sentences. Then listen to check your answers.

a) The briefcase is *in front of the television* .

b) The keys are in the hand bag .

c) The wallet is under the newspaper .

d) The umbrella is bihind the wastebasket

e) The comb is next to the hairbrush

f) The notebooks are on the dictionare .

10 LOST ITEMS

Pair work   You're late for work, and you need the things below.
Ask and answer the questions.

a) Where is my briefcase?
b) Where is my address book?
c) Where are my credit cards?
d) Where is my driver's license?
e) Where is my pen?
f) Where are my glasses?
g) Where is my umbrella?

> ▶ **Interchange 2: Find the differences**
> Look at two pictures of a room on page IC-3 and find the differences.

11 INSTRUCTIONS 🔲

1   Listen, and follow these instructions.

a) Pick up your book bag or your handbag.
b) Put it on your desk.
c) Take out your English book.
d) Put it next to your desk.
e) Take out your wallet.
f) Put it under your desk.
g) Take out a notebook.
h) Put it in front of your desk.

2   *Pair work*   Give your partner instructions. Use **in**, **on**, **under**,
next to, **behind**, and **in front of**. Then follow your partner's instructions.

3 Where are you from?

1 SNAPSHOT

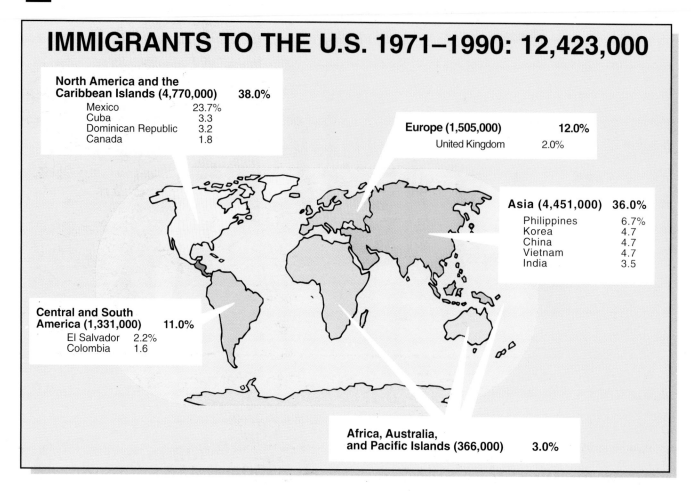

IMMIGRANTS TO THE U.S. 1971–1990: 12,423,000

North America and the Caribbean Islands (4,770,000) 38.0%

Mexico	23.7%
Cuba	3.3
Dominican Republic	3.2
Canada	1.8

Europe (1,505,000) 12.0%

United Kingdom	2.0%

Asia (4,451,000) 36.0%

Philippines	6.7%
Korea	4.7
China	4.7
Vietnam	4.7
India	3.5

Central and South America (1,331,000) 11.0%

El Salvador	2.2%
Colombia	1.6

Africa, Australia, and Pacific Islands (366,000) 3.0%

Are there immigrants in your country? ....
Where are they from? ....

2 WORD POWER

Class activity   Name two more countries from each region.

Europe ['juə rep]

....

....

Africa ['æf rikə]

....

....

Asia [ˈei/ə]

....

....

North America and the Caribbean [nɔː θ] [əˈm erikə]

....

....

Central and South America [ˈsentrəl ənd sauθ əˈmerikə]

....

....

3 CONVERSATION 🔲

1 Listen and practice.

Mark: Where are you from, Laura?
Laura: Well, my whole family is in the United
States now, but we're from Costa Rica
originally.
Mark: Oh, so you're from South America.
Laura: Actually, Costa Rica isn't in South
America. It's in Central America.
Mark: Oh, right. My geography isn't very good!

2 Listen to the rest of the conversation.

a) Where is Mark from?
b) Where is his country?

4 GRAMMAR FOCUS: Statements with *be* 🔲

I'm ₰(еетъ)	I'm not ₰ не (еетъ)	OR: ₰ не (еетъ)
You're	You're not	You aren't [аːнт]
He's	He's not	He isn't [iznt]
She's from Costa Rica.	She's not from El Salvador.	She isn't
It's	It's not	It isn't [aːnt]
We're	We're not	We aren't [aːnt]
They're	They're not	They aren't

1 *Pair work* Complete the sentences as in the example.
Compare answers with your partner.

a) Costa Rica is in Central America. *It's not* in South America.
b) My family is from Korea. We're in the U.S. now, Теперь [нау]
but *we're* from the U.S. originally.
c) Your glasses are on the table. *It's* over there,
next to the newspaper.
d) Hi, Sarah – oh, I'm sorry! *You're not* Sarah. Your name is Susan.
e) Where is my driver's license? *It's* in my wallet! Where is it?
f) Katherine and I aren't in your class. *We're* in Mrs. Lee's class.
g) Mr. Ho isn't from Hong Kong. *He's* from Singapore.

2 Complete the conversations. Then practice them.

A: Where _is_ Laura Sánchez from –
South America?
B: No, she _'s not_ from South America.
she's from Costa Rica.
A: Oh. So _she's_ from Central America.

A: Keiko, where _are_ you and Kenji from?
B: _We're_ both from Japan. [boud] oba
A: Oh, _are_ you from Tokyo?
B: No, we _aren't_ from Tokyo.
_we're_ from Kyoto.

A: Where _are_ you from, Mr. Park?
B: _I'm_ from the city of Pusan.
A: Where _is_ Pusan, exactly? точно
My geography _isn't_ very good.
B: Pusan _is_ in Korea.

---

5 **CONVERSATION** 🔊

Listen and practice.

Jack: Is this your newspaper?
Marta: Yes, it is. Here, take it.
Jack: Oh, but it isn't in English.
Marta: It's in Spanish. Spanish is my
native language.
Jack: Really? Are you Spanish?
Marta: Actually, I'm not. I'm from
Mexico.
Jack: Oh, so you're Mexican.
That's interesting.

16

6 COUNTRIES AND NATIONALITIES 🔊

Country	Nationality
They're from **Korea**.	They're **Korean**.
She's from **Mexico**.	She's **Mexican**.

1 Listen and practice. Notice the stressed syllables.

America	**Amer**ican	**Spain**	**Span**ish
Mexico	**Mex**ican	**Swe**den	**Swed**ish
Korea	**Kor**ean	**Ire**land	**Ir**ish
Canada	**Cana**dian	**Chi**na	**Chin**ese
Hungary	**Hung**arian	**Por**tugal	**Por**tuguese
Brazil	**Brazil**ian	**Ja**pan	**Japa**nese

2 Listen and underline the stressed syllables.
Then practice the words.

Colombia	Colombian	India	Indian
Egypt	Egyptian	Cambodia	Cambodian
England	English	Turkey	Turkish
Italy	Italian	Venezuela	Venezuelan
Poland	Polish	Vietnam	Vietnamese
Lebanon	Lebanese	Peru	Peruvian

3 *Pair work*   Complete the dialogues with the correct country or nationality. Then practice them.

A: I'm from Hungary.
B: Oh, so you're Hungarian.

A: Is Mr. Lee from Korea?
B: No, he's not from Korea. He's from China. [t͡ʃaɪnə]

A: Are you Vietnamese?
B: No, I'm not from Vietnam. I'm from Cambodia.

A: Your newspaper is in Spanish.
B: Yes, it's a _____ newspaper. I'm from Mexico.

A: We're from Peru.
B: Oh, so you're Peruvian.
A: That's right.

A: Are you from Japan?
B: Yes, we're Japanese.

4 *Class activity*   Guess the country for each nationality.

Country	Nationality	Country	Nationality
Nepal	Nepalese		Cuban
	Bolivian		Sudanese
	Panamanian		New Zealander
	Indonesian	France / Paris	French

верх листа TOP (handwritten)

7 LANGUAGES 🔊

THE TOP 10 LANGUAGES OF THE WORLD	THE 6 OFFICIAL LANGUAGES OF THE UNITED NATIONS
1. Chinese	1. Arabic
2. English	2. Chinese
3. Hindi	3. English
4. Spanish	4. French
5. Russian	5. Russian
6. Arabic	6. Spanish
7. Bengali	
8. Portuguese	
9. Japanese	
10. German	

What is your native language? ....

What is the official language of your
   country? ....

1 *Class activity*   What are the official languages of these countries?
What is another country with the same language?

A: German is the language of Austria.
B: German is the language of Germany, too.

a) Austria ....   d) Morocco ....
b) Brazil ....   e) New Zealand ....
c) Chile ....

2 *Pair work*   What do you think these languages are?

A: I think this is Spanish.
B: Yes, it's Spanish.

a) *(испанский — handwritten)*

> Yo soy un hombre sincero
> De donde crece la palma,
> Y antes de morirme quiero
> Echar mis versos del alma.

b) *(французск — handwritten)*

> Longtemps, je me suis
> couché de bonne heure.
> Parfois, à peine ma bougie
> éteinte, mes yeux se
> fermaient si vite que je
> n'avais pas le temps de
> me dire : « Je m'endors. »

c) *(Китаец — handwritten)*

> 原因は味？安全？

d) *(Японец — handwritten)*

> 夜思
> 林前明月光。
> 疑是地上霜。
> 举头望明月，
> 低头思故乡。

e)

> Очень просто. По окончани
> Казанского авиационного институ
> ждала распределения. Могли направи
> инженером на завод или младшим нау
> ым сотрудником в НИИ — бумажки г

f) *(немецкий — handwritten)*

> Eine Revolution raschelt durch die Republik:
> Jährlich drei Milliarden Fax-Seiten decken
> Privathaushalte und Unternehmen ein.

g) *(португальск — handwritten)*

> Para além do seu valor clínic
> medicamentos modernos
> proporcionam muitas vezes um
> eficácia de valor acrescentado
> para os cuidados de saúde.

низ листа bottom основание (handwritten)

8 LISTENING 🔲

Antonio, Mei-Ling, and Monique meet for the first time. Where are they from?
What are their native languages?

	Country	*Nationality*	*Language*
a) Antonio	....	....	....
b) Mei-Ling	....	....	....
c) Monique	....	....	....

9 GRAMMAR FOCUS: Questions and short answers with *be* 🔲

Are you from Canada?
Yes, I am.
No, I'm not.

Is Mary from New Zealand?
Yes, she is.
No, she's not. (No, she isn't.)

Is this handbag from Korea?
Yes, it is.
No, it's not. (No, it isn't.)

Are you and Lisa Chinese?
Yes, we are.
No, we're not. (No, we aren't.)

Are they from Japan?
Yes, they are.
No, they're not. (No, they aren't.)

1 Match the questions and the answers. Then practice with a partner.

a) Is your first name Jennifer? ....

b) Are you Michael Lynch? ....

c) Is English your native language? ....

d) Are these your keys? ....

e) Are you and your family from the United States? ....

f) Are your credit cards in your wallet? ....

1) No, they're not. My keys are different.
2) Yes, we are. We're from San Francisco.
3) Yes, it is. And my last name is Wan.
4) No, it's not. It's Japanese.
5) Yes, they are. They're in my wallet next to my driver's license.
6) No, I'm not. I'm David Bloom.

▶ **Interchange 3: Geography quiz**
Turn to pages IC-6 and IC-7 for a quiz on monuments in Europe, Africa, and Asia.

2 *Pair work* Write five questions to ask your partner. Then take turns asking questions.

4 Clothes and weather

1 SNAPSHOT

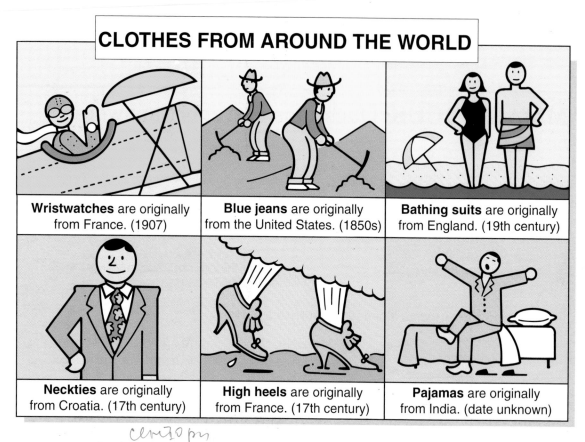

CLOTHES FROM AROUND THE WORLD

Wristwatches are originally from France. (1907)

Blue jeans are originally from the United States. (1850s)

Bathing suits are originally from England. (19th century)

Neckties are originally from Croatia. (17th century)

High heels are originally from France. (17th century)

Pajamas are originally from India. (date unknown)

What clothes are originally from your country? ....

2 COLORS 🔲

1 Listen and practice.

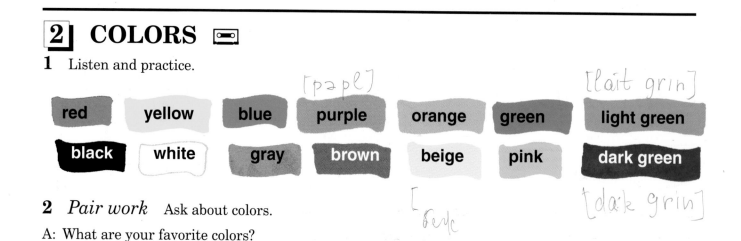

| red | yellow | blue | purple | orange | green | light green |

| black | white | gray | brown | beige | pink | dark green |

2 *Pair work* Ask about colors.

A: What are your favorite colors?
B: My favorite colors are green and purple.

3 WORD POWER: Clothes 🔊 *клуз приг одежда*

1 What color are these things? Listen and practice.

The suit is gray. The blouse is white . . .

suit [sjut]   blouse [blauz]   skirt [skät]   dress [dres]

slacks [slæks]   shirt [ʃət]   tie [tai]   coat [kout]

shorts [ʃɔːts]   running shoes [rʌniŋ ʃuːs]   hat [hæt]   boots [buːts]

scarf [skaf]   T-shirt [Ti-ʃət]   shoes [ʃuːs]

2 *Pair work*   Ask and answer questions about the clothes.

A: What color is the suit?
B: It's gray.

A: What color are the slacks?
B: They're light brown.

3 *Pair work*   Fill in the chart with words from pages 20 and 21.
Add two more words to each list.

Clothes for warm weather	Clothes for cold weather
....	....
....	....
....	....
....	....
....	....

4 CONVERSATION 📼

Listen and practice.

Susan: Uh-oh.
Peter: What's the matter?
Susan: It's snowing, and it's very cold.
Peter: Well, you're wearing a coat.
Susan: But I'm not wearing boots!
And it's thirty-two degrees.
Peter: That's zero degrees Celsius!
That's really cold.
Susan: So let's take a taxi.
Peter: Great idea. Come on!

5 GRAMMAR FOCUS: Present continuous;
and, but, so 🔊

I'm	I'm **not**	
You**'re**	you **aren't**	
She**'s** wearing a coat, but	she **isn't**	wear**ing** boots.
We**'re**	we **aren't**	
They**'re**	they **aren't**	

It's snowing, **and** it's very cold.

I'm wearing a coat, **but** I'm not wearing boots.

It's very cold, **so** let's take a taxi.

1 Complete these sentences with the information below. Then listen and practice.

a) She's running, so ...*she's wearing running shoes. and a sports pink suits*

b) He's driving, but ...*he isn't wearing his glasses. It's not comfortable without eyeglasses He can't see wee. It's very dangero*

c) We're walking in the snow, but ...*we aren't walkin wearing boots*

d) She's swimming, and ...*she's wearing a green bathing suit.*

e) They're playing tennis, but ...*they aren't wearing tennis shoes.*

f) It's snowing, and ...*I'm taking a walk upony mbaerzs*

1) ... I'm taking a walk.
2) ... we aren't wearing boots.
3) ... she's wearing running shoes.
4) ... they aren't wearing tennis shoes.
5) ... she's wearing a green bathing suit.
6) ... he isn't wearing his glasses.

It's rainy
It's r

Notice the spelling of the continuous verb form:		
wear	=	**wearing**
swim	=	**swimming** (+ m)
drive	=	**driving** (– e)

It's snowy - murws cneew to take a bus eger glasowy con
It's snowing, - uper cneez

2 *Pair work*   Complete the sentences about each picture. Compare answers with a partner.

a) We _'re wearing_ bathing suits, but
we _aren't swimming_ .
(wear, swim) *to relaxing, reading
listening to music*

b) He _'s driving_ , and
she _'s running_ .
(drive, run)

c) It _'s snowing_ , and
they _'re swimming_ .
(snow, swim)

d) They _'re playing_ basketball, so
they _'re wearing_ shorts.
(play, wear)

e) He _'s working_ today, so
he _'s wearing_ a suit and tie.
(work, wear)
*What is he doing?
What does he do?*

f) She _'s carring_ a briefcase, but
she _'s carring_ a handbag.
(carry, carry)

3 *Class activity*   Write three true sentences and three false
sentences about your classmates. Then read them to the class.
Your classmates say "right" or "wrong."

A: Su Hee is wearing black shoes.
B: That's right.

A: Juan is wearing a suit and tie.
B: That's wrong. He's wearing a suit,
   but he isn't wearing a tie.

6 NUMBERS 🔲

Listen and practice.

11	eleven	21	twenty-one	40	forty
12	twelve	22	twenty-two	50	fifty
13	thirteen	23	twenty-three	60	sixty
14	fourteen	24	twenty-four	70	seventy
15	fifteen	25	twenty-five	80	eighty
16	sixteen	26	twenty-six	90	ninety
17	seventeen	27	twenty-seven	100	one hundred
18	eighteen	28	twenty-eight	101	one hundred and one
19	nineteen	29	twenty-nine	102	one hundred and two
20	twenty	30	thirty		

7 TEMPERATURES

1 Match the Fahrenheit and equivalent Celsius temperatures.
Practice with a partner.

A: What is .... degrees Fahrenheit?

B: It's .... degrees Celsius.

a) ninety
b) one hundred and four
c) seventy-two
d) three
e) fifty
f) eighty-six
g) sixty-six

g) nineteen
c) e) twenty-two
...... ten
f) thirty
a) thirty-two
...... forty
d) sixteen below zero

2 *Pair work* Ask and answer questions.

A: What is the temperature in .... ?
B: It's .... Celsius. (It's .... Fahrenheit.)

Temperatures around the world for February 1

city	temperature F	C	city	temperature F	C
Buenos Aires	82	28	São Paulo	89	32
Moscow	12	-11	Sydney	85	29
Paris	46	8	Taipei	64	18
Quebec City	3	-16	Tokyo	43	6
San Francisco	60	15	Vancouver	41	5

°F °C

110   45
100   40
90   35
80   30
70   25
60   20
50   15
40   10
30   5
20   0
10   -5
0   -10
-10   -15
      -20
      -25

25

8 WHAT'S THE WEATHER LIKE? 📼

Listen and practice.

It's spring.
It's raining. It's cool.
It's fifty degrees.

It's summer.
It's warm and sunny.
It's eighty.

She's sunbathing
(a bop - eerega)

It's summer.
It's very hot and humid. *Crakns*
It's ninety-five.

He's fanning himself
He's sweating no

It's fall. *A leafs are falling*
It's windy.
It's cool. It's cloudy.

Gone with the wind.
about

It's winter.
It's very cold. *it's snowy*
It's five degrees. *[digzi:]*

It's winter.
It's snowing.
It's thirty-two degrees.

cemege

9 LISTENING 📼

Listen to the weather reports for the cities below. Write the temperature
and check off the weather conditions.

	Temperature	hot	warm	cool	cold	sunny	cloudy	raining	snowing
a) Sapporo (Japan)	−20° C				✗				✗
b) Bangkok (Thailand)	+28° C		✗			✗			
c) Miami (U.S.A.)	20° C			✗			✗		
d) Rio de Janeiro (Brazil)	25° C	✗						✗	

Conditions — *Челябинск*

10 CLOTHES AND WEATHER

1 *Pair work* What's the weather like in these pictures?
What are the people wearing? Write three sentences about each picture.
Then compare sentences with your partner.

a) *It's cold. It's 28 degrees. She's wearing . . .*

a

28°F   -2°C

©SAM
VIVIANO
1994

b 95°F   32°C

c 81°F   27°C

2 *Pair work* Ask and answer these questions.

What's the weather like today in your city?
What are you wearing today?

▶ **Interchange 4: What's the weather like?**

What's the weather like in North and South America on February 1? Look at the map on page IC-5.

Review of Units 1–4

1 Prepositions of place

Group work   Identify two items from your bag, briefcase, or wallet.
Give them to your classmates. Your classmates put the items in a different
place. Ask where the items are.

A: This is my driver's license.
B: These are my keys . . .

A: Where is my driver's license?
B: It's under your chair . . .

2 Listening

Tim is looking for things in his room. His mother is
helping him. Listen and mark the location of each item
in the picture.

a)

b)

c)

d)

e)

He's teenager. He's in his teens.

3 Same or different?

Pair work   Choose two classmates. Are their clothes the same or different?
Write five sentences and then compare with a partner.

Same	Different
Juan and Victor are both	Juan is wearing boots,
wearing blue jeans.	but Victor is wearing shoes.

4 Instructions

Pair work   Complete the instructions below. Read the instructions to your partner. Follow your partner's instructions.

a) Close ....
b) Open ....
c) Take out ....
d) Say ....
e) Go ....

f) Write ....
g) Spell ....
h) Pick up ....
i) Put ....
j) Carry ....

5 What's the question?

1   Match the questions and the answers. Then practice with a partner.

✓ a) What's your name? ......6.....
   b) What's this called in English? ....8....
✓ c) How do you spell *calculator*? ....1....
✓ d) Where is my English book? ....
✓ e) Where are you from? ......5.....
✓ f) What color are your shoes? ...10....
✓ g) What's the weather like today? ...3....
✓ h) What's the temperature today? ...4....
   i) What is your teacher wearing today? ...7...
✓ j) What's your telephone number? ...2...

· 1) It's C-A-L-C-U-L-A-T-O-R.   c
· 2) It's 555-3493.   j
· 3) It's windy and it's raining.   g
· 4) It's eighty-five degrees Fahrenheit.   h
· 5) We're from Thailand.   e
· 6) It's Sarah Smith.   a
· 7) He's wearing a suit and tie.
   8) It's a driver's license.
   9) It's under your chair.   d
- 10) They're black.   f

2   *Pair work*   Ask and answer the same questions. Answer with personal information.

6 What's strange about this picture?

strange – странный

Pair work   Find five strange things in the picture. Write a sentence about each one. Compare your sentences with a partner.

> A woman is swimming, and she's wearing a blouse and a hat.

fur coat

29

5 What are you doing?

1 CONVERSATION 🔊

Listen and practice.

Deborah: Hello?
John: Hi, Deborah! This is John. I'm calling [kɔliŋ]
      from Australia.
Deborah: What are you doing in Australia? [dʌiŋ] сделать
John: I'm attending a conference in Sydney [ə'tendiŋ]
      this week. Remember? [ri'membə]
Deborah: Oh, right. What time is it there? [ðɛə]
John: It's 10:00 P.M. And it's four o'clock
      in Los Angeles, right?
Deborah: Yes – four o'clock in the morning.
John: 4:00 A.M? I'm really sorry.
Deborah: That's OK. I'm awake now. [ə'weik] [nau]

2 WHAT TIME IS IT? (1) 🔊

1 Listen and practice.

What time is it?
It's five o'clock in the morning. [klɔk]
It's 5:00 A.M.

It's seven o'clock in the
   morning. [mɔːniŋ]
It's 7:00 A.M.

It's twelve o'clock.
It's noon. [nuːn]
(It's 12:00 noon.) полдень

It's four o'clock in the
   afternoon. ['aftə'nuːn]
It's 4:00 P.M.
время после полудня

It's seven o'clock in the
   evening. ['iːvniŋ]
It's 7:00 P.M.

It's twelve o'clock at night.
It's midnight. полночь
(It's 12:00 midnight.)

2 Say it another way.

a) It's eight o'clock in the evening. *It's 8:00 P.M.*
b) It's twelve o'clock at night. *It's 12:00 P.M.*
c) It's three o'clock in the afternoon. [It's 3:00 PM]
d) It's 3:00 A.M. *It's three o'clock in the morning*
e) It's 9:00 A.M. *It's nein o'clock morning*
f) It's 4:00 P.M. *It's four o'clock in the afternoon*

30

3 GRAMMAR FOCUS: Present continuous: *What + doing* ▭

1 Listen and practice.

What is Victoria doing?
She's sleeping.

What is Juan doing?
He's getting up.

What are Sue and Tom doing?
They're having breakfast.

What is Celia doing?
She's going to work.

What are Paul and Ann doing?
They're having lunch.

What is Boris doing?
He's working.

book keeper
an

What is Permsak doing?
He's having dinner.

What is Jim doing?
He's watching television.

What are you doing?
I'm . . .

2 *Pair work* Ask and answer questions about the pictures.

a) What time is it in Los Angeles?
b) What is Victoria doing?
c) Where are Sue and Tom?
d) What are they doing?
e) Who is working right now?
f) What is Juan wearing?
g) What is he doing?
h) Who is carrying a briefcase?

31

4 LISTENING 🔊

It's 7:00 P.M. in New York. Sue and Tom are calling their friends in different cities. What time is it in Bangkok? Tokyo? Brasília?

▶ **Interchange 5: Time zones**

Talk about what people are doing in different cities of the world. Turn to page IC-8.

5 SNAPSHOT

TELLING TIME

alarm clock   clock radio   watch   digital watch   sports watch

oy (ноль)

How many watches or clocks do you own? ....
What kind are they? ....

6 WHAT TIME IS IT? (2) 🔊

1 Listen and practice.

It's five minutes after three.   It's ten minutes after five.   It's 9:30 (nine thirty).
It's 3:05 (three-oh-five).   It's 5:10 (five-ten).   *noef afternine*

It's a quarter to eleven.   It's a quarter after seven.   It's twenty-five to eleven.
It's 10:45.   It's 7:15.   It's 10:35.

2 *Pair work*   Look at these clocks. What time is it?

A: What time is it?
B: It's twenty minutes after two. (It's 2:20.)

half to 5

7 CONVERSATION 🔲

Listen and practice.

Mr. Ford: Hey! Are you getting dressed?
Mrs. Ford: Yes, I am.
Mr. Ford: Why? What time is it?
Mrs. Ford: It's a quarter to eight. I'm going to work.
Mr. Ford: But it's Saturday.
Mrs. Ford: I'm working on Saturday mornings this month. Are you getting up?
Mr. Ford: No, I'm not. I'm staying in bed.
Mrs. Ford: OK. See you at noon.
Mr. Ford: If I'm awake.

Mr.Ford is unemployed He doesn't have a job
He has many chores.

8 PRONUNCIATION 🔲

1 Listen to the intonation of statements and yes/no questions.

I'm getting up now. ↘   Are you getting up? ↗

He's having breakfast. ↘   Is she having breakfast? ↗

2 Now listen to these sentences. Are they yes/no questions or statements? Circle **Q** or **S**.

a) Q̶ S   c) Q S̶   e) Q S̶

b) Q S̶   d) Q̶ S   f) Q̶ S

9 LISTENING: Saturday chores 🔲

Listen to the sounds of some Saturday chores. Number the pictures from 1 to 4.

a) ....   b) *9:00 AM* ....   c) *12:00* ....   d) *10 AM* ....

vacuuming

washing the dishes

shopping

cleaning the house

He's   chores

10 GRAMMAR FOCUS: Present continuous: yes/no questions 🔊

Are you getting up?	Is he having breakfast?	Is she going to work?	Are they working?
Yes, I am.	Yes, he is.	Yes, she is.	Yes, they are.
No, I'm not.	No, he isn't.	No, she isn't.	No, they aren't.

1 *Pair work* Ask and answer questions about the Fords. Use the verbs.

A: What time is it?
B: It's a quarter to eight.
A: Is Mrs. Ford getting dressed?
B: Yes, she is.
A: Is Mr. Ford getting dressed?
B: No, he isn't. He's sleeping.

It's half to 12.
Is Mrs Ford working?
Yes, she is.
Is Mr. Ford working?
No, he isn't. He's having breakfast

It's a quarter after 2
Mrs. Ford cleaning the house?

get dressed?

work?

clean the house?

[kli:n]

shop?   *reading*

go to the movies? *theater*
кино (опптанса).

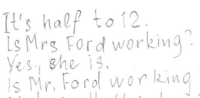

dance? *She's tired*

2 *Pair work* Write five more questions about the Fords.
Then ask and answer the questions with a partner.

> It's 2:15. Is Mr. Ford sleeping? . . .

11 READING 🔊 *naparpap, abzay*

1   Find the picture for each paragraph.

1

2

3

4

It's Saturday!
What are you doing today?

a) c   b) .... a   c) .... a   d) .... b

CHRIS JOHNSON: What am I doing? I'm shopping for summer clothes. This bathing suit is great. I'm also looking for sandals. I'm getting ready for a vacation at the beach.	TERRY RIVERA: We're working in the garden today. We're planting flowers and pulling weeds. This is our favorite thing to do on a Saturday.	STACY CHEN: My friend and I are just driving around and looking at people. We're not doing anything special. But we're having fun.	PAT EDWARDS: I'm just sitting outdoors, in a café. And I'm having coffee, of course. I'm reading a great book. It's a love story. Uh-oh. It's starting to rain.

2   Add these sentences to the paragraphs.

a) But we're feeling tired now.
b) And I'm not carrying an umbrella.
c) I'm looking for sunglasses, too.
d) We're listening to music on the car radio.

3   *Group work*   Imagine you and your classmates are together on a Saturday. Write five sentences about what you are doing.

We're listening to the radio . . .

5 GRAMMAR FOCUS: Present tense statements

Regular verbs

I	**live**	I	**don't live**	[dount]
You	**live**	You	**don't live**	
He/She	**lives** in the suburbs.	He/She	**doesn't live** in the city.	[dʌzt]
We	**live**	We	**don't live**	
They	**live**	They	**don't live**	

Irregular verbs

I **have** a car.
My wife **has** a car, too.
We both **go** to work by car.
My son **goes** to school by bus.
I **do** my work in an office.
My son **does** his work at school.

1 Complete Julia's sentences with the correct verb form.
Then listen to check your answers.

a) I *live* (live, lives) with my parents.
b) We *live* (live, lives) downtown.
c) My parents *have* (has, have) an apartment.
d) I *walk* (walk, walks) to work.
e) I *don't* (don't, doesn't) need a car.
f) My mother *doesn't* (don't, doesn't) walk to work.
g) She *uses* (use, uses) public transportation.
h) She *takes* (take, takes) the subway.
i) My father is retired, so he *doesn't* (don't, doesn't) have a job.
j) But he *does* (do, does) a lot of work at home.
k) He also *watches* (watch, watches) television.
l) I *have* (has, have) a brother and a sister.
m) My sister *has* (has, have) a husband and three children.
n) They *live* (live, lives) in a house in the country.
o) The children *go* (go, goes) to school by bus.
p) My brother *has* (has, have) an apartment in the city.
q) He *lives* (live, lives) alone.
r) He *doesn't* (don't, doesn't) have a car.
s) He *uses* (use, uses) public transportation.
t) He *goes* (go, goes) to work by bus.

2 *Pair work* Write five sentences about you and your family.
Use the sentences above as a model. Then compare with a partner.

> I live with my parents . . .

3 *Class activity* Are you and your partner the same
or different? Tell the class.

"I live with my parents, but Keiko lives alone.
We both drive to class . . ."

6 SPELLING AND PRONUNCIATION:
Third person singular *s* 🔊

1 Listen and practice. Notice the spelling.

	s = /s/		*s = /z/*		*s = /ɪz/*		*irregular*
take	take**s**	live	live**s**	watch	watch**es**	do	do**es**
walk	walk**s**	go	go**es**	use	use**s**	say	say**s**
speak	speak**s**	carry	carr**ies**	close	close**s**	have	ha**s**

2 *Pair work* Read any verb from list A. Your partner says the verb from list B.

A	B		A	B		A	B
wear	wears		swim	swims		close	closes
play	plays		work	works		write	writes
walk	walks		snow	snows		say	says
run	runs		rain	rains		erase	erases
go	goes		open	opens		do	does

7 CONVERSATION 🔊

1 Listen and practice.

Matthew: Let's go to the park on Sunday.
Amy: OK, but not too early. I get up early on weekdays,
        so I sleep in on the weekend.
Matthew: What time do you get up on Sundays?
Amy: At ten o'clock.
Matthew: Oh, that's early. I get up at noon.
Amy: Do you have breakfast?
Matthew: Sure. I eat breakfast every day.
Amy: Then let's meet at Harry's Restaurant at
        one o'clock. On Sundays, they serve breakfast
        all day . . . for people like us.

2 Listen to the rest of the conversation.

a) What time does Amy get up
   on weekdays?
b) What time does Matthew get up
   on weekdays?

39

8 GRAMMAR FOCUS: Present tense questions

Do you get up early on Sundays? What time **do you get** up?	No, **I get** up late. At noon.
Does she eat breakfast in the morning? What time **does she eat** breakfast?	Yes, **she eats** breakfast at work. At nine o'clock.
Do they go to work together? What time **do they go** to work?	Yes, **they go** together every day. At a quarter to eight.

1 Unscramble the questions to complete the conversations.
Then practice with a partner.

A: I get up early every day.
B: .... ?
   (you get what time up do)
A: At 6:00 A.M.

A: .... ? *сказала*
   (Julia does alone live)   *вся поставленном*
B: No, she lives with her parents. *маток*

A: Sophia and Jason go to school by bus.
B: .... ?
   (does come the bus what time)
A: It comes at eight o'clock.

A: .... ?
   (have you every breakfast day do)
B: Yes, I have breakfast with my family.

Time expressions

every day
every morning

on Sundays
on weekdays

in the morning
in the afternoon

at nine o'clock

2 *Pair work*   Write the answers to these questions.
Then ask and answer the questions with a partner.

a) What time do you get up?
b) Do you have breakfast every day?
c) Do you read the newspaper in the morning or in the evening?
d) What time do you leave for work?
e) How do you go to work? Do you drive? Do you take the bus?
f) What time do you have lunch? Do you go to a restaurant?
g) Do you take a break in the afternoon?
h) What time do you go home?
i) Do you have dinner with your family?
j) Do you watch television in the evening?
k) Do you read in the evening?

▶**Interchange 6:
Class survey**
Find out more about your classmates. Turn to page IC-9.

9 DAYS OF THE WEEK 📼

1   Listen and practice.

Sunday	Monday	Tuesday	Wednesday	Thursday	Friday	Saturday

2 *Pair work*   Ask and answer questions.

a) What do you do on Saturdays? On Sundays? On Mondays?
b) What time do you go to bed on weekdays? On the weekend?
c) Do you have a job? What days do you work?
d) What days do you have English class?
e) What is your favorite day of the week? Why?

Weekdays	Weekend
Monday	Saturday
Tuesday	and
Wednesday	Sunday
Thursday	
Friday	

10 READING 📼

1   One piece of information (one word) in each paragraph is incorrect.
Can you find it? Listen to check your answers.

раннешние

What's your work schedule?

Randall Kelly   Restaurant cook

"I get up at 5:00 A.M., get dressed, and drive to work. The restaurant opens at 6:00 A.M. sharp. We serve breakfast until eleven and lunch until three. Then I go home. I go to bed at around nine, and hope that the telephone doesn't ring. Luckily, I don't work on Saturdays or Sundays, I only work on weekends."

этоардееа
Andrea Morris Flight attendant
иного

"Sometimes I go to work at 5:00 A.M., and sometimes I go at 5:00 P.M. Sometimes I leave the house on Monday and don't come home until Wednesday. I often work on weekends. My job is interesting, but my schedule is regular. And I don't see my husband enough."

уоитогио

sen
Rob Jefferson   Rock musician

"I go to work at ten o'clock in the evening, and I play until 3:00 A.M. I take a break at midnight, though. *soy* After work I have dinner at an all-night restaurant. Then I take a taxi home. I go to bed at five in the morning and sleep until two in the morning. I only work three nights a week – Friday, Saturday, and Sunday."

2   Answer the questions.

a) Who gets up early? Who gets up late?
b) Who works at night? Who works during the day?
c) Who works on weekends? Who works on weekdays?
d) Find one thing you like about each person's schedule.

to leave оставить

3   Write five sentences about your schedule.

sharp – остро
b точно точно – точно = exactly

41

7 Does the apartment have a view?

1 SNAPSHOT

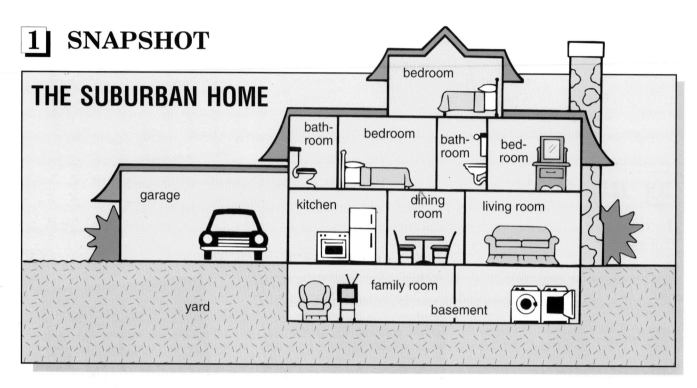

THE SUBURBAN HOME

- bedroom
- bath-room
- bedroom
- bath-room
- bed-room
- garage
- kitchen
- dining room
- living room
- yard
- family room
- basement

What rooms do houses have in your country? ....
What rooms do apartments have in your country? ....

2 CONVERSATION

Listen and practice.

Linda: Guess what! I have a new apartment.
I'm moving in this weekend.
Chris: Really? Do you need help?
Linda: Well, yes, I do. Thank you!
Chris: No problem.

Chris: So what is the apartment like?
How many rooms does it have?
Linda: Well, it has a bedroom, a kitchen,
and a living room. And a big closet.
Chris: That's great. Where is it?
Linda: It's on Lakeview Drive.
Chris: Oh. Does it have a view?
Linda: Yes, it does. It has a great view
of my neighbor's apartment!

3 GRAMMAR FOCUS: Present tense questions and short answers 🔲

Do you **live** in an apartment?
Yes, I **do**.
No, I **don't**.

Does the apartment **have** a view?
Yes, it **does**.
No, it **doesn't**.

Do the bedrooms **have** closets?
Yes, they **do**.
No, they **don't**.

How many rooms **does** the apartment **have**?
It **has** four rooms.

1 Complete the conversation with verbs. Then practice with a partner.

Linda: ___Do___ you ___live___ in an apartment?
Chris: No, I ___don't___ . I ___live___ in a house.
Linda: What is it like? ___Does___ it ___have___ a yard?
Chris: Yes, it ___does___ . And it's next to the river.
Linda: That sounds great. ___Do___ you ___live___ alone?
Chris: No, I ___don't___ . I ___live___ with my parents and my sisters.
Linda: How many sisters ___do___ you ___have___ ?
Chris: I ___have___ four.
Linda: That's a big family. ___Do___ you ___live in___ a big house?
Chris: Yes, we ___do___ . It ___has___ ten rooms.
Linda: Ten rooms! How many bedrooms ___does___ it ___hes___ ?
Chris: It ___hes___ four.
Linda: ___Do___ you ___have___ your own bedroom?   *оун собственная*
Chris: Yes, I ___do___ . I'm really lucky.   *рем*
Linda: ___Does___ your bedroom ___have___ a view of the river?
Chris: No, it ___doesn't___. It's in the basement.

2 *Pair work* Write five questions to ask your partner about his or her house or apartment. Then ask your questions.

> *Do you live in an apartment? . . .*

4 LISTENING 🔲

Listen to people describe their house or apartment. Number the pictures from 1 to 4.

a) ___3___   b) ___4___   c) ___1___   d) ___2___

5 DREAM HOUSE

1   Write a description of your dream house.

Where is your dream house?
How many rooms does it have?
What are the rooms?
What else does it have?

> My dream house is in the country.
> It has twenty rooms . . .

2   *Pair work*   Ask your partner about his or her dream house.

A: Does it have a swimming pool?
B: Yes, it does.

6 CONVERSATION 🔊

Listen and practice.

Chris: This apartment is very nice.
Linda: Yes, but I need some furniture.
Chris: What do you need?
Linda: Well, there's a table in the kitchen,
        but there aren't any chairs.
Chris: And there's no sofa in the living room.
Linda: Right. There are only two armchairs.
Chris: So, let's go to a yard sale next weekend.
Linda: That's a great idea!

7 WORD POWER

modern - современной
old fashioned - старомодный
ancient - [эйшент] - старинная

1 You need furniture for your apartment. Choose things at the yard sale.
Make a list for each room.

For the kitchen I need

kitchen	dining room	living room	bedroom
	столовая	*современная*	
dresser [dresə]	table	sofa	bed
stove [stouv]	chairs [tʃɛəs]	grandfather clock	mirror ['mirə]
refrigerator	curtains	coffee table	rug [rʌg]
microwave oven	grandfather clock	rug [rʌg]	curtains [kətns] *штор*
(майкровайв)		curtains [kətans]	picture
		picture	dresser
		armchairs [am tʃɛəs]	
		television	

2 Add three more things to each list.

3 *Pair work*   Compare lists with your partner. What do you need?

"For the kitchen, I need a stove, a refrigerator, and . . ."

dishwasher
посудомоет. маш.

plants - цветы в горшках
flowers - цветы живые
artificial flowers - искусствен. цветы

45

8 GRAMMAR FOCUS: *there is/there are* 🔊

There's a table in the kitchen.
There's no sofa in the living room.
There are some armchairs in the living room.
There aren't any chairs in the kitchen.

There's = There is

1 *Pair work*   Say what furniture Linda has in each room.
Your partner says what furniture is missing.

A: There's a mirror in the bedroom.
B: There's no dresser in the bedroom.

2 *Pair work*   Write five sentences about things
you have or don't have in your classroom.
Compare sentences with your partner.

5 предложений

> There are twenty desks in the room.
> There aren't any pictures on the wall . . .

▶**Interchange 7:
Find the differences**
Compare the two apartments on
page IC-10.

9 PRONUNCIATION: /ð/ and /θ/ 🔲

1 Listen and practice.

/ð/   /θ/   /ð/   /ð/   /θ/   /θ/
There are **th**irteen rooms in **the** house. **The** house has **th**ree ba**th**rooms.

2 Find three more words with /ð/ and three more words with /θ/.

/ð/	/θ/
....	....
....	....
....	....

10 READING 🔲

любимый
['feivərit]

What's your favorite room?

Joseph Landi:

My favorite room is the kitchen. We
have a big kitchen, with a modern stove
and refrigerator. There's a big dining
table, so we always eat dinner here
together. I cook every evening and
weekend. My children cook, too, but
they only use the microwave oven.

Liz Johnson:

My favorite room is my bedroom.
It's my "private study." I have a desk, a
bookcase, and a computer in here. I also
have a bed, of course. It's the room
where I read, study, play computer
games, and sleep.

Susan Stern:

The living room is my favorite room.
It's the room where I relax at night.
There are some beautiful pictures on the
wall. There's a comfortable sofa. I sit on
the sofa and watch TV every evening.
Sometimes I listen to music on the
stereo system.

1 Complete the chart. What do these people do in their favorite room?
What are the good features of the room?

	Favorite room	**Activities**	**Good features**
Joseph Landi	kitchen	cook, dinner	all family eat together
Liz Johnson	bedroom	read, study, play computer	private study
Susan Stern	living room	watch TV, listen music	relax at night

2 Write five sentences about your favorite room.

47

1 WORD POWER: Jobs 📼

1 Identify the occupations of the people in the pictures. Use the words in the list. Then listen and practice.

cashier	judge	pilot	security guard
cook/chef	lawyer	police officer	singer
doctor	musician	receptionist	waiter
flight attendant	nurse	salesclerk	waitress

She's a receptionist . . .

a) *receptionist* b) doctor c) nurse   d) musician e) singer f) musician

g) cook h) waiter i) waitress   j) pilot k) flight- l) attendant)

m) judge n) lawyer o) police officer p) salesclerk q) security guard r) cashier

2 *Pair work* Who works at the places below? Choose occupations from page 48.
Add one more occupation to each list.

A: A doctor works in a hospital.
B: A nurse works in a hospital, too.

in a hospital	in an office	in a store	in a hotel
....	....	....	....
....	....	....	....
....	....	....	....

3 *Class activity* Ask and answer questions about occupations.

Who . . . a) wears a uniform?
　　　　 b) stands all day?
　　　　 c) sits all day?
　　　　 d) handles money?
　　　　 e) talks to people?
　　　　 f) works hard?
　　　　 g) works at night?
　　　　 h) carries a gun?

A: Who wears a uniform?
B: Police officers wear a uniform.
C: Security guards . . .

2 **CONVERSATION**

Listen and practice.

Rachel: Where does your brother work?
Angela: He works in a hotel.
Rachel: Oh. What does he do, exactly?
Angela: He's a chef in a French restaurant.
Rachel: That's interesting. My boyfriend
　　　　 works in a hotel, too.
Angela: Is he a chef?
Rachel: No, he's a security guard, but he
　　　　 doesn't like the work. So he's looking
　　　　 for a new job.

3 GRAMMAR FOCUS: Present tense: Wh-questions with *do* 🔲

Where do you work?	Where does she work?	Where do they work?
I work in a hotel.	She works in a store.	They work in a hospital.
What do you do there?	**What does she do** there?	**What do they do** there?
I'm a receptionist.	She's a cashier.	They're nurses.

1 Complete these sentences. Put the sentences in order to make three conversations. Listen to check your answers.

a) __3__ Really? What _does_ (do/does) she _do_ (do/does) there?
__2__ She _works_ (work/works) in a hospital.
__4__ She _is_ (am/is) a doctor.
__1__ Where _does_ (do/does) Elizabeth _work_ (work/works)?

b) __3__ Oh? And what _do_ (do/does) you _do_ (do/does) there?
__1__ Where _do_ (do/does) you _work_ (work/works)?
__4__ I _'m_ (am/is) a salesperson. I _sell_ (sell/sells) computers.
__2__ I _work_ (work/works) in a department store.

c) __4__ He _repairs_ (repair/repairs) TVs.
__1__ What _does_ (do/does) Tom _do_ (do/does)?
__2__ He _works_ (work/works) in an electronics store.
__3__ What _does_ (do/does) he do there, exactly?

2 *Class activity*   Ask three classmates their occupations. Then tell the class.

Where do you work?
What do you do, exactly?

"Mrs. Chen is a cashier. She works in a department store . . ."

4 PRONUNCIATION: Falling intonation 🔲

1 Listen and practice.

A: Where do you work?

B: I work in a store.

A: What do you do?

B: I'm a salesclerk.

2 Listen to the conversations again in exercise 1 of the Grammar Focus. Practice them using falling intonation.

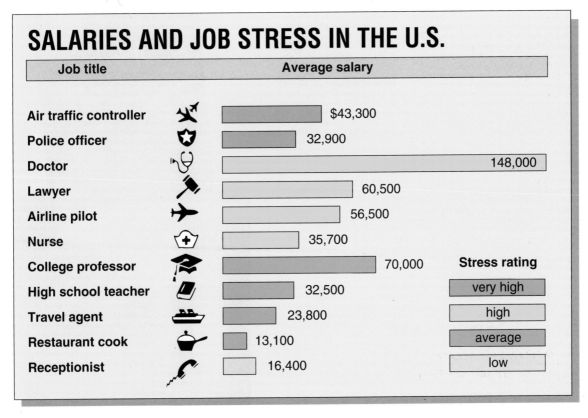

5 SNAPSHOT

SALARIES AND JOB STRESS IN THE U.S.

Job title	Average salary
Air traffic controller	$43,300
Police officer	32,900
Doctor	148,000
Lawyer	60,500
Airline pilot	56,500
Nurse	35,700
College professor	70,000
High school teacher	32,500
Travel agent	23,800
Restaurant cook	13,100
Receptionist	16,400

Stress rating
- very high
- high
- average
- low

What other professions are stressful? ....
What other professions have high salaries? ....

6 CONVERSATION

Listen and practice.

Richard: Hi, Stephanie. I hear you have a new job.
Stephanie: Yes, I'm teaching math at Lincoln High School.
Richard: So how do you like it?
Stephanie: Well, the salary is a little low, but the students are nice. How are things with you?
Richard: Not bad. You know I'm an air traffic controller now.
Stephanie: Now that's an exciting job!
Richard: Yes, but it's very stressful.

7 **GRAMMAR FOCUS:** Adjectives 🔲

be + adjective [ædʒɪktɪv] *прилаг.*		**Opposites**	
A lawyer's salary **is high.** [haɪ]		high	low
A police officer's job **is dangerous**.		safe	dangerous
		interesting	boring
adjective + noun		pleasant	unpleasant
A lawyer has **a high salary**.		easy	difficult
A police officer has **a dangerous job**.		relaxing	stressful

1   Say it another way.

a) A nurse's job is interesting. *A nurse has an interesting job.*
b) A computer programmer's job is difficult.
c) A doctor's salary is high.
d) A lawyer's job isn't easy.
e) A chef's job is pleasant.
f) A security guard's job is dangerous.

2 *Pair work*   Complete the sentences with adjectives.
Then compare answers with your partner.

a) A cashier has ~~a easy job~~ .
b) A salesclerk's job is ~~interesting~~ .
c) A police officer's job isn't ~~safe~~ .
d) A musician has ~~a~~ .
e) A flight attendant's job is ~~stressful~~ .
f) A receptionist doesn't have ~~dangerous job~~.

3 *Class activity*   Find two jobs for each category.
Do you and your classmates agree?

an exciting job	a high salary
....	....
....	....
a difficult job	a dangerous job
....	....
....	....
a boring job	a low salary
....	....
....	....
an easy job	a stressful job
....	....
....	....

▶ **Interchange 8:**
The perfect job
Find out what you want in
a job. Turn to page IC-11.

A: A doctor has an exciting job.
B: A doctor's job isn't exciting. It's stressful.
C: I agree. I think a doctor has a stressful job.

8 LISTENING 🔲

Listen to these women talk about their jobs. Number the pictures from 1 to 4.

a).........

b).........

c).........

d).........

9 READING 🔲

1 Read the article, and then complete the chart.

What do you do, exactly?

Anthony Duran, telephone operator

As a directory assistance operator, I give out hundreds of telephone numbers every day. I sort of like talking to people all day. I earn around $20,000 a year. But I don't feel very secure – a lot of operators are losing their jobs because of automation. Computers do everything these days. So I'm studying to be a computer programmer at night school.

Robert Fine, travel agent

My clients are all business travelers. I make plane, hotel, and car reservations for them. My annual salary isn't very high – only $24,000 – but I like my job. It's pretty secure, because travel is a growing field. Also, I often travel in order to learn about cities, hotels, airlines, and tours. And when I do, everything is free – the plane tickets, the hotel rooms, etc.

Kimberly Evans, physical therapist

In my job, I mainly work with athletes who have sports injuries. Sometimes the athletes are famous, and that's always exciting. My salary is good – $38,000 a year – and I always have a lot of patients. Doctors are too busy to do physical therapy these days, and they're happy to give the work to specialists like us.

Job	Salary	What they do	One good thing about the job
....	....	....	....
....	....	....	....
....	....	....	....

2 Write five sentences about your job, or a job you would like to have.

I'm an accountant . . .

Review of Units 5–8

1 Listening 🔊

Pair work   Victoria is calling friends in different parts of the world.
Where are they? What time is it there? What are they doing? Complete the chart.

Victoria   Sue   Juan   Jim

	City	*Time*	*Activity*
Sue	....	....	....
Juan	....	....	....
Jim	....	....	....

2 Different responses

Pair work   Write two different answers to these questions.
Use the present continuous. Then practice with a partner.

A: What are you doing? Are you watching television?
B: No, I'm . . .

A: Are you going to school? What courses are you taking?
B: . . .

A: Is Maria at school today?
B: No, she's . . .

A: What's that noise? Is it the people in the next apartment?
B: Yes, they're . . .

A: Are you going to the party? What are you wearing?
B: . . .

3 | Habits

Write eight sentences about yourself. Then compare with a partner.

a) Name two things you do in the morning.
b) Name two things you don't do in the morning.
c) Name two things you do on the weekend.
d) Name two things you don't do on the weekend.

> I have breakfast in the morning . . .

4 | Comparisons

Class activity   What are some differences between these things?
Write four sentences about each pair, using the expressions in the box.
Compare your answers with your classmates.

a) a house and an apartment
b) the city and the country

> A house has a yard, but an apartment . . .

> It has . . .
> It doesn't have . . .
> There is . . .
> There's no . . .
> There are . . .
> There aren't . . .

5 | What's the question?

[handwritten: c) Are you like your job?]

1   Look at these answers. What are the questions? Write the questions down.

[handwritten: b) What does you do, exactly?]

Where do you work?

a) I work in a store.

b) I'm a sales clerk.

c) I really like my job.

d) I live in an apartment downtown.

e) My apartment has a kitchen, a bathroom, and a living room.

f) I need a sofa, a rug, and a carpet.   *[handwritten: [ka:pit]]*

g) I think my English class is great!

i) I get up at 6:00 A.M. every morning.

j) It's four o'clock in the morning!

h) I go to class by subway.

k) I'm watching television right now.

[handwritten: h) How are you go to class?   k) What are you going?]

2   *Pair work*   Ask and answer the questions with a partner.
Use personal information.

[handwritten: d) Where are you live?   e) What has your apartment?   f) What are you need?   g)   i) What time do you get up?]

55

9 I love strawberries!

1 WORD POWER 🔲

Match the foods to the words in the chart. Then listen and practice.
Add two more foods to each category.

These are bananas . . .

BASIC FOODS

handwritten annotations:
и плоды фрукты [fruit]
овощи [vedʒitəbl]
накрохмаленне [statʃi]
gəapu молочные мясо [deəzi] [miːt]
риба

Fruit	Vegetables	Starches	Dairy	Meat and fish
c apples	h broccoli	m beans [biːns]	s butter	w beef [biːf] *ровяг*
a bananas [bənɑnə]	f carrots [kæɹəts]	l bread [bɹed]	r cheese [tʃiːz]	u chicken [tʃikin]
e mangoes	c green beans	k pasta	g eggs [eg]	v lamb *ягне* [ɔtʃiːʃ]
b oranges [ɔɹindʒ]	j peppers [pepə]	o potatoes [pəteitou]	p milk	y salmon [sæsmɔn]
d strawberries	g tomatoes [	h rice [zɑis]	t yogurt	x shrimp [ʃɹimp]

56

2 GRAMMAR FOCUS: Countable vs. uncountable 🔲

Countable			Uncountable	
singular	**plural**		**singular only**	
an apple	apples	I'm eating **an apple**.	yogurt	I'm eating **yogurt**.
a carrot	carrots	**Apples** are my favorite fruit.	beef	**Yogurt** is delicious.
a potato	potatoes	I like **apples**.	broccoli	I love **yogurt**.

1   Divide the words in the chart on page 56 into two lists.

countable		*uncountable*	
apples	....	broccoli	....
....	....	....	....
....	....	....	....

2   *Pair work*   Cover the chart on page 56 and identify the foods.

A: I think these are carrots.
B: Right. And this is broccoli.

3   Complete these sentences with **is** or **are**. Listen to check your answers.

a) Strawberries ......*in*........ my favorite fruit. I love strawberries!
b) I think mangoes ......*the*........ delicious.
c) Green beans ....*are*........ my favorite vegetable.
d) Broccoli ....*is*.......... very good for you.
e) I think cheese ....*is*...... awful. I hate cheese!
f) Chicken ......*is*........ my favorite meat.

4   *Pair work*   Write responses to the items below.
Then compare information with a partner.

a) Name two foods you hate.
b) Name two foods you love.
c) Name three foods that are good for you.
d) What's your favorite fruit?
e) What's your favorite vegetable?
f) What's your favorite meat?

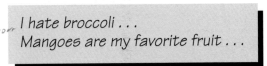

I hate broccoli . . .
Mangoes are my favorite fruit . . .

fruit and vegetable market

A: I hate broccoli. Do you like broccoli?
B: Yes, I do. But I hate peppers. Do you like peppers?
A: No, I don't . . .

57

3 PRONUNCIATION: Word stress 📼

Listen and notice the stress in these words. Find one more example of each pattern.

stress on first syllable	*stress on second syllable*
apple	po**ta**toes
strawberries	to**ma**toes
....	....

4 CONVERSATION 📼

Listen and practice.

Charles: What do we need for the barbecue?
Anne: Well, we need hamburger meat and hot dogs.
Charles: We have some hamburger in the freezer,
         but we don't have any hot dogs.
Anne: Right, and there aren't any buns.
Charles: Do we need any soda?
Anne: Yes, we do. Let's buy some soda and
         some lemonade, too.
Charles: All right. And how about some potato salad?
Anne: Great idea! Everyone likes potato salad.

5 LISTENING 📼

Listen to the rest of the conversation. Which desserts do Charles and Anne choose? Complete their shopping list.

cake   pie   cookies
ice cream   chocolate

SHOPPING LIST
hot dogs
buns
drinks
— — soda
— — lemonade
potato salad
dessert
— —
— —

6 GRAMMAR FOCUS: *some, any* 🔊

Affirmative statements	Questions and negative statements	
We need **some vegetables**.	Do you want **any carrots**?	We don't need **any carrots**.
We need **some meat**.	Do you want **any chicken**?	We don't need **any chicken**.
We need **some**.	Do you want **any**?	We don't need **any**.

1 Complete the conversation with **some** or **any**.
Then practice with a partner.

Charles: Let's not buy potato salad. Let's make ....
Anne: OK. So we need ...*some*... potatoes and
...*some*... mayonnaise.
Charles: Is there ...*any*... mayonnaise at home?
Anne: No, we need to buy ....
Charles: OK. Oh, we need ...*some*... onions, too.
Anne: I don't want ...*any*... onions in the
salad. I hate onions!
Charles: Then let's buy ...*some*... celery. That's
good in potato salad.
Anne: Good idea. And ...*some*... carrots, too.
Charles: Sure. There are .... over there.

onion - лук
celery - сельдерей

2 *Pair work* What do you need from the
supermarket today? Make a list. Then compare with
a partner.

A: I need some bread.
B: I don't need any bread, but I need some rice.

7 SNAPSHOT

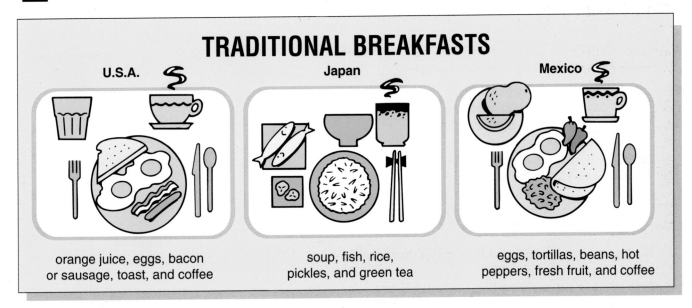

TRADITIONAL BREAKFASTS

U.S.A.

orange juice, eggs, bacon
or sausage, toast, and coffee

Japan

soup, fish, rice,
pickles, and green tea

Mexico

eggs, tortillas, beans, hot
peppers, fresh fruit, and coffee

What is a traditional breakfast in your country? ....
What is your favorite meal? ....

8 CONVERSATION 🔲

Listen and practice.

Sarah: Let's have breakfast together on
          Sunday.
Kumiko: OK. But why don't you come to my
          house? On Sundays my family has
          a Japanese-style breakfast.
Sarah: Really? What do you have?
Kumiko: We usually have fish, rice, and soup.
Sarah: Fish? Now that's interesting.
Kumiko: We sometimes have salad, too. And
          we always have green tea.
Sarah: Well, I don't often eat fish for
          breakfast, but I love to try new things.

9 GRAMMAR FOCUS: Frequency adverbs 🔲

I	**always**	have breakfast.	Do you	**usually**	have tea?
	usually			**ever**	
	often				
	sometimes		I don't	**usually**	have tea.
	seldom			**often**	
	never			**ever**	

100 %	**always**
	usually
	often
	sometimes
	seldom
0 %	**never**

(handwritten margin notes):
всегда [ɔːlwəz]
[juːʒʊəli]
[ɔfn] часто иногда
[seldən] редко
[nevə] никогда
ever [evə] всегда

1 *Pair work*   Add the adverbs to the sentences. Then practice
the conversation with a partner.

A: What do you have for breakfast? (usually)
B: Well, I have eggs, bacon, and toast on Sundays. (often)
A: Do you eat breakfast at work? (ever)
B: Yes, I have breakfast at my desk. (sometimes)
A: Do you eat rice for breakfast? (ever)
B: I don't have rice. (often)

2 *Pair work*   Add three questions of your own. Then ask
and answer questions with a partner.

a) Do you usually have breakfast in the morning?
b) What do you usually eat?
c) Do you ever eat meat or fish for breakfast?
d) Do you ever go to a restaurant for breakfast?
e) Do you always drink the same thing for breakfast?
f) Name one thing you never have for breakfast.

10 **READING** 📟

1 Match the letters in the picture to the paragraphs.

The Hamburger

You probably think that the hamburger is a typical American food. Americans often have a hamburger for a quick lunch or snack. But do you know that the favorite American "fast food" actually comes from many different countries?

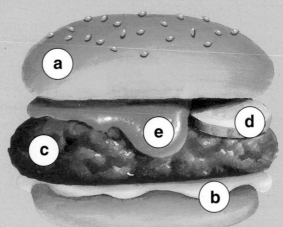

.... The **hamburger** is made of beef, not ham. The idea of chopping meat into very small pieces comes from Turkey. The name *hamburger* comes from the town of Hamburg in Germany.

.... The **pickle**, or pickled cucumber, comes from Eastern Europe. It is popular in Poland and Russia.

.... The word **ketchup** comes from China. "Ke-tsiap" is the Chinese name for a sauce made of pickled fish and spices. The first recipe for tomato ketchup is in a 1792 American cookbook.

.... **Mayonnaise**, sometimes called "mayo," is a yellow-white sauce made of eggs, oil, and lemon juice. It comes from the Spanish island of Minorca, but its name is French. Mayonnaise is also used as a dressing for salads.

.... The **bun** is a kind of bread. It comes from an English recipe, and the sesame seeds on top come from the Middle East.

So, the "American" hamburger is a truly international meal!

2 Answer these questions.

a) What different countries does the hamburger come from? Make a chart.

ingredients	places of origin
....	....
....	....

b) What other things do people put on hamburgers? What do you like on a hamburger?

c) What do you need to make your favorite sandwich, snack, or dessert? Write about it.

▶ **Interchange 9: Planning a picnic**
Turn to page IC-12 and plan a picnic with three other students.

My favorite sandwich is . . . To make the sandwich, you need . . .

10 Can you swim very well?

1 SNAPSHOT

SOME OLYMPIC SPORTS

And countries with the most gold medals in these sports since 1952

Winter Games

speed skating
Former Soviet Union: 24

downhill skiing
Austria: 8

Summer Games

free-style swimming
United States: 34

marathon
Ethiopia: 3

What is your favorite winter sport? ....
What is your favorite summer sport? ....
What is your favorite Olympic sport? ....

2 CONVERSATION 🔈

Listen and practice.

Katherine: It's really hot. Let's go to the pool.
Philip: OK, but I can't swim very well.
Katherine: Well, I can't, either. I can only swim ten laps.
Philip: Ten laps? I can't even swim across the pool!
Katherine: But I can't dive at all. Can you dive?
Philip: Well, yes, I can. In fact, I can dive quite well.
Katherine: So, let's go. I can teach you how to swim, and you can teach me how to dive.

3 GRAMMAR FOCUS: *can* with abilities 🔲

I				you				I		
You				I				you		
She	**can**	swim.	**Can**	she	**swim** very well?	Yes,	she	**can**.
He	**can't**			he		No,	he	**can't**.
We				we			we	
They				they			they	

1 Katherine is talking about what she **can** and **can't** do.
Listen and practice.

a) I .... draw.

b) I .... write poetry.

c) I .... fix a car.

d) I .... play the piano.

e) I .... sing very well.

f) I .... cook very well.

2 *Pair work*   Complete the sentences above with
your own information. Compare with a partner.
Use **too** or **either**.

A: I can cook.
B: I can cook, too. I can't draw.
A: I can't draw, either. But I can sing very well.
B: I can't sing.

3 *Group work* Make a circle. Find out what special talents your classmates have. Ask about these abilities.

classmate's name								
....	☐	☐	☐	☐	☐	☐	☐	☐
....	☐	☐	☐	☐	☐	☐	☐	☐
....	☐	☐	☐	☐	☐	☐	☐	☐
....	☐	☐	☐	☐	☐	☐	☐	☐

Juan: Keiko, can you dance?
Keiko: Yes, I can. Tai-lin, can you dance?
Tai-lin: No, I can't. Can you dance, Ana? . . .

---

4 **PRONUNCIATION:** *can* and *can't* 🔲

1 Listen and practice. Notice that **can** is reduced.

/kən/   /kænt/
I **can** play the piano, but I **can't** sing very well.

2 *Pair work* Read a sentence from list A or B. Your partner says "A" or "B."

A

I can dance.
He can draw.
She can sing.
They can skate very well.

B

I can't dance.
He can't draw.
She can't sing.
They can't skate very well.

---

5 **CONVERSATION** 🔲

Listen and practice.

Matthew: What's your new girlfriend like?
Philip: Katherine? Well, she's good at languages.
Matthew: Does she know how to speak Spanish?
Philip: She knows how to speak Spanish *and* Japanese.
Matthew: Wow!
Philip: And she's good at sports, too. She knows
              how to play tennis and basketball.
Matthew: That's terrific.
Philip: But there's one thing she's not good at.
Matthew: What's that?
Philip: She's not good at remembering things.
              We have a date, and she's an hour late!

6 WORD POWER: Sports 🔊

1 Listen and practice.

They're playing basketball.

soccer

baseball

football

basketball

volleyball

golf

tennis

Ping-Pong

2 Now complete the chart. Add two more sports to each category.

team sports	*individual sports*
basketball	

3 *Pair work*   Ask a partner about sports abilities.

A: Do you know how to play basketball?
B: Yes, I do. (No, I don't.)

7 GRAMMAR FOCUS: *be good at; know how to* 🔲

> **Is** your girlfriend **good at** sports?
> She**'s good at** team sports.
>
> She **knows how to play** basketball,
> but she **doesn't know how to play** baseball.

1 *Pair work*   Add five more questions.
Then interview a partner.

a) Are you good at languages?
b) Do you know how to speak Japanese, Spanish, or Russian?
c) What languages can you speak fluently?
d) Are you good at sports?
e) Do you know how to play soccer?
f) Are you good at winter sports?
g) Do you know how to ski or ice-skate?
h) Are you good at card games?
i) What card games do you know how to play?
j) Are you good at board games?
k) Do you know how to play chess?
l) What board games do you know how to play?
m) Are you good at video games?
n) .... ?
o) .... ?
p) .... ?
q) .... ?
r) .... ?

2   Write five sentences about your partner.
Read them to the class.

> *Keiko is good at languages. She can speak Spanish fluently. She isn't good at sports, but . . .*

a board game: Scrabble

chess

a card game

a video game

---

8 LISTENING 🔲

Listen to questions and choose the best response.

a) ☐ No, I can't.
   ☐ No, I don't.

b) ☐ Yes, I can.
   ☐ Yes, I do.

c) ☐ Yes, I can.
   ☐ Yes, I do.

d) ☐ Yes, I can.
   ☐ Yes, I do.

e) ☐ No, I don't.
   ☐ No, I can't.

f) ☐ No, I don't.
   ☐ No, I can't.

9 READING 🔊

Amazing animals

Do you know that the kangaroo can't walk at all – but it can travel at 40 miles an hour! This amazing animal is very good at jumping. It can jump 20 feet at a time. An adult kangaroo is only five feet tall, but it can jump over a car.

The camel can live without water for one week. It can walk over 200 miles in the desert without drinking water. It can do this because it has three stomachs that hold water. And the hump on its back holds fat, so the camel can live without food for a long time, too.

The chimpanzee is a very intelligent animal that is good at learning language. A chimpanzee can learn to use sign language, but it can't always use correct grammar. For example, a chimpanzee can use sign language to say, "Me want banana now," but not, "I want a banana now, please."

1 Read about these animals and then fill in the chart.

	Can	*Can't*
Kangaroo	....	....
Camel	....	....
Chimpanzee	....	....

2 Do you know something interesting about an animal? Write about it.

A giraffe can clean its eyes and ears with its tongue . . .

▶ **Interchange 10: Hidden talents**

Learn about your classmates' special abilities. Turn to page IC-13.

8 CELEBRATIONS

Pair work   What are these people doing? What are they going to do? Write four sentences about each picture, using the expressions in the box below. Then compare sentences with a partner.

a) It's Jeremy's birthday . . .

b) It's New Year's Eve . . .

c) It's Jessica's high school graduation . . .

d) It's the Fourth of July in the U.S. . . .

blow out the candles	receive some presents
sing "Happy Birthday"	have a party
open the presents	wear special hats
shout "Happy New Year"	have a good time
kiss their friends	have a picnic
listen to a speech	cook food on the barbecue
receive a diploma	watch the fireworks

▶ **Interchange 11: Vacation plans**

Talk about your next vacation or a "dream" vacation. Turn to page IC-14.

9 READING 🔲

What are you going to do on your birthday?

Elena Buenaventura, Madrid, Spain:
"My twenty-first birthday is on Saturday, and I'm going to go out with some friends. To wish me a happy birthday, they're going to pull on my ear 21 times, once for each year. It's an old custom. Some people do it only once, but my friends are very traditional!"

Mr. and Mrs. Isai, Kyoto, Japan:
"My husband is going to be 60 tomorrow. In Japan, the sixtieth birthday is called *kanreki* – it's the beginning of a new life. The color red represents a new life, so we always give something red for a sixtieth birthday. What am I going to give my husband? I can't say. It's a surprise."

Sun Hee Shi, Taipei, Taiwan:
"Tomorrow is my sixteenth birthday. It's a special birthday, so we're going to have a family ceremony. I'm probably going to receive some money in 'lucky' envelopes from my relatives. My mother is going to cook noodles – noodles are for a long life."

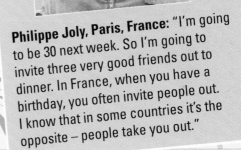

Philippe Joly, Paris, France: "I'm going to be 30 next week. So I'm going to invite three very good friends out to dinner. In France, when you have a birthday, you often invite people out. I know that in some countries it's the opposite – people take you out."

1 Read the four paragraphs. Then correct these statements.

a) To celebrate her birthday, Elena is going to pull on her friends' ears.
b) Sun Hee is going to cook some noodles on her birthday.
c) On his birthday, Mr. Isai is going to buy something red.
d) Philippe's friends are going to take him out to dinner on his birthday.

2 Do you have plans for your next birthday, or for the birthday of a friend or family member? What are you going to do? Write several sentences.

> *I'm going to be twenty-five on March 15th. I'm going to . . .*

73

12 What's the matter?

1 SNAPSHOT

COMMON REASONS FOR MISSING CLASS

a cold   a stomachache   the flu   feeling sad or "blue"   a "bad hair day"

What are other reasons to miss class? ....
Do you ever miss work or class? Why? ....

2 CONVERSATION 🔲

Listen and practice.

Brian: Hi, Victor. How are you?
Victor: Oh, I'm fine.
Brian: So, are you going to go to class tonight?
Victor: Maybe, but I don't think so.
Brian: Really? What's the matter?
Victor: I don't know. I'm just feeling a little sad.
Brian: Listen. Come with me to class, and after class we can go out for dinner.
Victor: Now that's a good idea. Thanks a lot, Brian. I'm feeling better already.

3 HEALTH PROBLEMS 🔊

1 Listen. Point to each body part.

Point to your head.

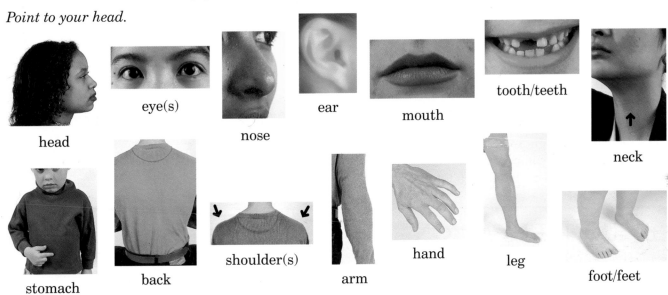

head

eye(s)

nose

ear

mouth

tooth/teeth

neck

stomach

back

shoulder(s)

arm

hand

leg

foot/feet

2 Listen and practice these conversations.

A: What's the matter?
B: I have a headache.
A: Oh, that's too bad.

A: What's wrong?
B: I have a sore throat.
A: Oh, I'm sorry to hear that.

A: How do you feel?
B: I feel terrible. I have a cold.
A: Well, I hope you feel better soon.

3 *Class activity* Take turns acting out the illnesses below or other health problems. Classmates guess what is wrong and give you sympathy.

A: Do you have a headache?
B: No, I don't.
C: Do you have an earache?
B: Yes, I do.
C: That's too bad!

a headache	the flu	a sore foot
a backache	a cold	a sore arm
a stomachache	a fever	a sore throat
an earache		

4 LISTENING 🔊

Listen to people talk about health problems. What's wrong with them?
Write the name of the body part where they have a problem.

a) ....

b) ....

c) ....

d) ....

e) ....

f) ....

5 PRONUNCIATION: Sentence stress 🔲

1 Listen to the stressed syllables in each sentence. Then practice the sentences.

What's the **mat**ter?
I have a terrible **head**ache.
I have a very sore **throat**.

2 *Class activity* Listen and underline the syllable with the strongest stress in each sentence. Then practice the conversation.

A: What's the problem?
B: I have a very high fever.
A: Are you taking some aspirin?
B: Yes, I am. And I'm drinking a lot of water.

6 CONVERSATION 🔲

Listen and practice.

Receptionist: Dr. Ryan's office.
Susan: Hello, this is Susan West. Can I make an appointment on Friday the 17th?
Receptionist: OK, Ms. West. In the morning or afternoon?
Susan: In the afternoon.
Receptionist: Can you come at 4:00 P.M.?
Susan: That's fine.

Dr. Ryan: And what's the problem, Ms. West?
Susan: I have a terrible backache. I can't even sit down.
Dr. Ryan: OK. Take these pills every four hours. Stay in bed this week. And don't lift heavy things.
Susan: Thanks, Dr. Ryan.

7 TIME EXPRESSIONS: *on, at,* and *in* 📼

in the morning	**on** Monday	**at** 10:00 A.M.
in the afternoon	**on** Monday morning	**at** two o'clock
in the evening	**on** Mondays	**at** noon
in June	**on** July 15th	**at** midnight
in December	**on** the 15th (of July)	**at** night
in the summer	**on** weekdays	
	on weekends	

Pair work   Complete the conversations. Then practice with a partner.

A: Are you free *on* Sunday? There's a party at Victoria's place.
B: Is the party *in* the afternoon?
A: No, it starts *at* 8:00 P.M.
B: But I never go to parties *on* Sunday nights. I go to work *at* 7:30 A.M. Monday.
A: But the party is *on* July 3rd. You don't work *on* the Fourth of July. It's a holiday.

A: Can I make an appointment *on* June? I'm free *on* Wednesdays.
B: Can you come *on* Wednesday the 7th?
A: *On* the 7th, I can only come *in* the morning.
B: I have an opening *at* ten *in* the morning.
A: Good. So the appointment is *on* Wednesday the 7th *at* 10:00 A.M.
B: That's right. See you then.

A: Can I have an appointment *on* Tuesday the 6th?
B: *In* the morning?
A: No, *in* the afternoon, please.
B: Can you come *at* three o'clock?
A: That's fine. So my appointment is *at* three o'clock *on* the 13th.
B: Well, no, it's *on* Tuesday the 6th. By the way, what's your problem?
A: I have trouble remembering things. When is my appointment again?

8 **GRAMMAR FOCUS:** Imperatives 🔊

Affirmative	Negative
Take these pills.	**Don't drink** coffee.
Stay in bed.	**Don't lift** heavy things.
	Don't forget your doctor's appointment.

1 What are these people saying? Choose from the sentences in the box.
Compare with a partner.

I have a headache.
I can't sleep at night.
My job is very stressful.
I have a fever.
I can't lose weight.
I have a stomachache.
There's no food in the house.

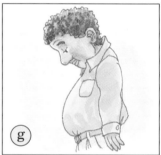

2 *Pair work* What is your advice for the people above?
Choose from the list below or think of your own advice.

A: I have a fever.
B: Take two aspirin . . .

Don't eat desserts.

Don't drink coffee or
tea in the evening.

Go out to a
restaurant.

Go to bed
and sleep.

Go home and relax.

Eat some toast and
drink some tea.

Don't go to work.

Take a hot bath
at night.

Take two aspirin and
drink a lot of water.

Don't eat any food
for a day.

Get some exercise
every day.

Go to a store and
buy some food.

Go to bed early
at night.

9 READING 📼

SECRETS OF A LONG LIFE

Sadie and Bessie Delany are sisters who live in Mount Vernon, New York. Sadie is 104 years old, and Bessie is 102. They tell their life story in a book called "Having Our Say: The Delany Sisters' First Hundred Years."
Here is some of their advice for living a long, healthy life.

* Get up early. The Delany sisters get up at 6:30 or 7:00 A.M.

* Have a good breakfast. The sisters eat oatmeal, half a banana, bran, and eggs with a little cheese.

* Exercise every day. The Delany sisters like to do yoga. They also walk every day.

* Eat lots of vegetables, especially garlic. Garlic is good for your health, even if it's not good for your breath!

BUT . . .

* **Don't** eat a lot of salt and fat. These things are bad for you.

* **Don't** get married! The sisters say, "We are still alive because we don't have husbands who worry us."

* **Don't** listen to the doctor. "Most doctors don't know what to do with us," Sadie says. "When something's wrong they say, 'You're still living, what do you expect?'"

1 Do you agree with Bessie and Sadie's advice? If you agree, write **yes**.
If you don't agree, write some advice of your own.

Eat lots of vegetables. ....
Don't get married. ....
Exercise every day. ....
Get up early. ....
Don't eat a lot of salt or fat. ....
Don't listen to the doctor. ....
Eat a lot of garlic. ....
Have a good breakfast. ....

2 Can you think of any more advice for living a long life?
Write at least five sentences like these:

> *Drink a lot of juice. Don't eat desserts.*
> *Don't . . .*

> ▶ **Interchange 12: Helpful advice**
> Turn to page IC-15 and give advice for some common problems.

13 Can you help me, please?

1 WORD POWER

1 Where can you buy these things? Match the items with the places. Then listen and practice.

You can buy books at a bookstore.

a) books ...5....

b) a fish dinner ....

c) carrots ....

d) stamps ....

e) a television ....

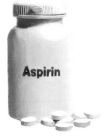

f) gasoline ....

g) aspirin ....

h) a magazine ....

1) a supermarket

2) a drugstore

3) a newsstand

4) a restaurant

5) a bookstore

6) a department store

7) a gas station

8) a post office

2 *Pair work*   Ask and answer these questions with a partner.

a) Where can you buy clothes?
b) Where can you have a hamburger?
c) Where can you buy furniture?
d) Name four places you can buy a magazine.
e) Who works at a department store? A restaurant?
f) Name three things you can buy at a newsstand.
g) Name three things you can buy at a drugstore.
h) Name five things you can buy at a supermarket.

2 PRONUNCIATION: Compound nouns 🔲

1   Listen and practice.

post office   **gas** station   **drug**store   **news**stand

2   Find four more expressions made of two words. Say them aloud.

....
....

3 CONVERSATION 🔲

Listen and practice.

Charles: Can you help me, please? Is there a public
          restroom near here?
Woman: I'm sorry, but I don't think so.
Charles: Oh, no! My son needs a bathroom.
Woman: Well, there's a department store on Grant
          Street. There are restrooms in the basement.
Charles: Where on Grant Street?
Woman: Between Second and Third Streets.
          The store is across from the hotel.
Charles: Thank you very much.
Woman: You're welcome.

4 LISTENING 🔲

What are these people going to buy? Where are they going to buy it?
Listen and complete the chart.

	What	*Where*
a) Sarah	....	....
b) Michael	....	....
c) Jennifer	....	....
d) Victor	....	....

5 GRAMMAR FOCUS: Prepositions of place 🔈

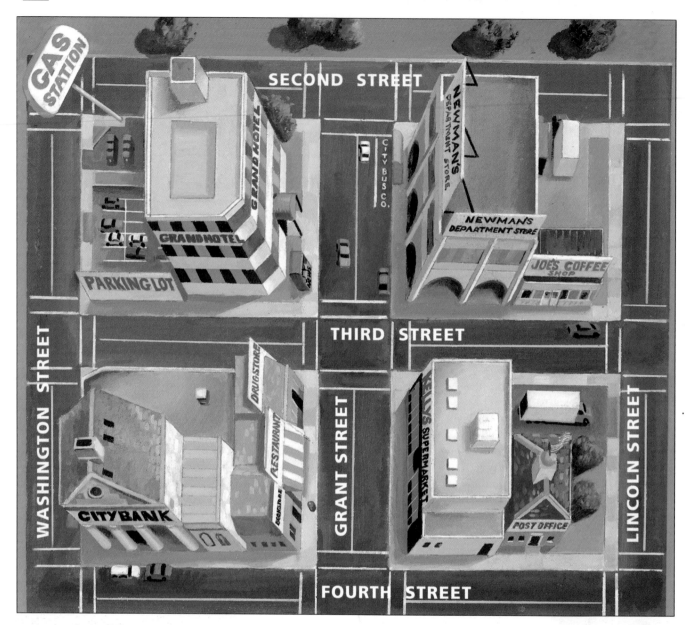

The department store is **on** Grant Street.
It's **between** Second and Third Streets.
It's **across from** the Grand Hotel.
There's a newsstand **in front of** the hotel.

There's a gas station **behind** the hotel.
The gas station is **on the corner of** Washington and Second.
The gas station is **next to** a parking lot.
The parking lot is **near** the City Bank.

1   Look at the map and complete the sentences.

a) There's a bus stop *in front of* the department store.
b) There's a parking lot .... the department store.
c) The parking lot is *behind* the Grand Hotel.
d) There's a gas station *next to* the parking lot.
e) There's a restaurant *on* Grant Street, *between* Third and Fourth Streets.
f) The restaurant is *between* a drugstore and a bookstore.
g) The bookstore is .... Grant and Fourth.

on the corner of

2 *Pair work* Look at the map on page 84 and complete the conversations. Then practice with a partner.

A: Excuse me, sir. Is there a restaurant _near_ here?
B: Well, there's a new restaurant _on_ Grant Street.
   It's _across from_ Kelly's Supermarket. But it's expensive.
A: Isn't there a coffee shop _on_ Third Street?
B: Yes, it's _on the_ Lincoln and Third.
   corner of

A: Excuse me, miss. Is there a gas station _on_
   Washington Street?
B: Yes, there is. It's _on the corner of_ Washington and Second.
A: So it's _behind_ the Grand Hotel.
B: Right. And it's _next to_ a big parking lot.

3 *Pair work* Ask and answer questions about your neighborhood.

A: Is there a bookstore near here?
B: Yes, there is. It's on Taylor Street, next to the post office.

---

6 LISTENING 📼

Look at the map on page 84 as you listen to these conversations.
Where are these people going?

a) .... b) .... c) ....

---

7 CONVERSATION 📼

Listen and practice.

Tourist: Excuse me, ma'am. How do I get to
St. Patrick's Cathedral?
Woman: Walk up Fifth Avenue to 50th Street.
St. Patrick's is on the right.
Tourist: Is it near Rockefeller Center?
Woman: It's right across from Rockefeller Center.
Tourist: Thanks. And what about the Empire State Building?
Is it far from here?
Woman: It's right behind you. Just turn around
and look up!

8 SNAPSHOT

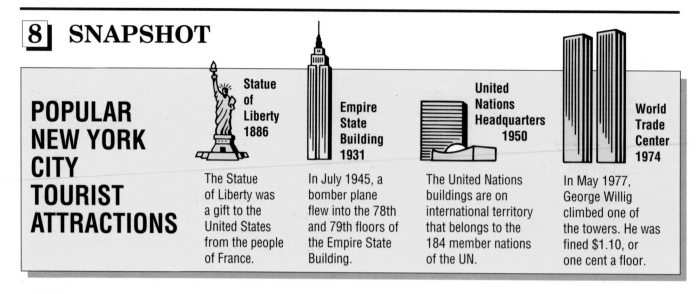

POPULAR NEW YORK CITY TOURIST ATTRACTIONS

Statue of Liberty 1886
The Statue of Liberty was a gift to the United States from the people of France.

Empire State Building 1931
In July 1945, a bomber plane flew into the 78th and 79th floors of the Empire State Building.

United Nations Headquarters 1950
The United Nations buildings are on international territory that belongs to the 184 member nations of the UN.

World Trade Center 1974
In May 1977, George Willig climbed one of the towers. He was fined $1.10, or one cent a floor.

Do you know any other tourist attractions in New York City? ....

What are some tourist attractions in your city? ....

9 DIRECTIONS 🔲

Walk **down** Fifth Avenue **for ten blocks.**
    up   **to 50th Street.**

Turn **right** at 50th Street.
    left

The building is **on the right**.
           on the left.

Follow the directions as you look at the map. What building are you going to?

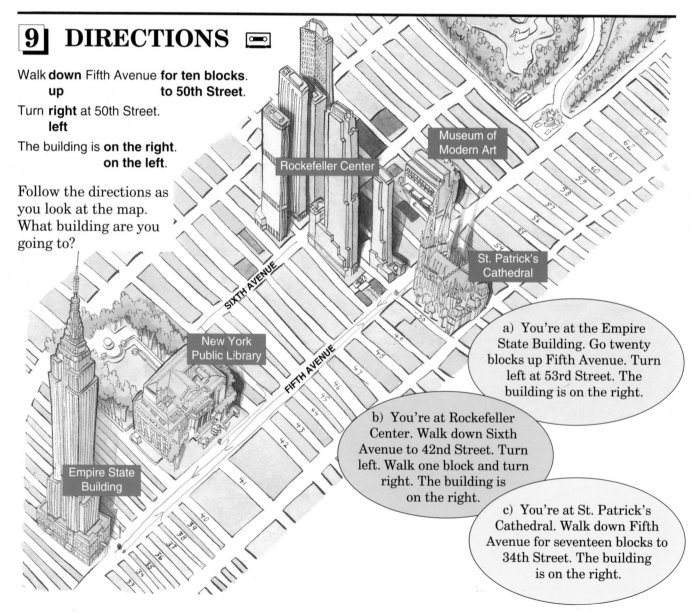

a) You're at the Empire State Building. Go twenty blocks up Fifth Avenue. Turn left at 53rd Street. The building is on the right.

b) You're at Rockefeller Center. Walk down Sixth Avenue to 42nd Street. Turn left. Walk one block and turn right. The building is on the right.

c) You're at St. Patrick's Cathedral. Walk down Fifth Avenue for seventeen blocks to 34th Street. The building is on the right.

10 READING 🔘

1 As you read, follow the directions on the map on page 86.

A walk up Fifth Avenue

Start your tour at the **Empire State Building,** on Fifth Avenue between 33rd and 34th Streets. This building has 102 floors. Take the elevator to the 102nd floor for a great **view** of New York City.

Walk up Sixth Avenue to 49th Street. You're standing in the middle of the 19 buildings of **Rockefeller Center**. Turn right on 49th Street, walk another block, and turn left. You're in Rockefeller Plaza. In the winter, there's a **rink** where you can ice-skate.

Now walk seven blocks up Fifth Avenue to the New York Public Library. The entrance is between 40th and 42nd Streets. This library holds over 10 million books. Behind the library is **Bryant Park**. In the summer, there's an outdoor café, and at lunch hour, there are free **music concerts**.

Right across from Rockefeller Center on Fifth Avenue is **St. Patrick's Cathedral**. It's modeled after the cathedral in Cologne, Germany. Go inside the cathedral and leave the noisy city behind. Look at the beautiful blue **windows**. Many of these windows come from France.

2 Where can you do these things?

a) Where can you have a view of the city?
b) Where can you go skating in the winter?
c) Where can you listen to music outdoors?
d) Where can you sit quietly indoors?

3 Write answers to the questions above.
Use information about your town.
Write two sentences for each question.

> In my town, you can listen to music in a park next to the river . . .

▶ **Interchange 13: Directions**

Give directions in a town.
Student A turns to page IC-16 and Student B turns to page IC-18.

15 Where were you born?

1 SNAPSHOT

FAMOUS AMERICANS BORN IN OTHER COUNTRIES

Albert Einstein
(1879–1955)

▸ Scientist
▸ Born in Germany
▸ Published *Theory of Relativity* in 1915

I. M. Pei (1917–)

▸ Architect
▸ Born in China
▸ Buildings: Pyramid in the Louvre, Paris; Bank of China in Hong Kong

Martina Navratilova (1956–)

▸ Tennis player
▸ Born in the former Czechoslovakia
▸ Winner of Wimbledon, 1978 –79, 1982–87, 1990

Name famous people in your country who came from another country. ....

2 CONVERSATION

Listen and practice.

Chuck: Were you born in the U.S., Melissa?
Melissa: No, I wasn't. I came here in 1992.
Chuck: How old were you?
Melissa: I was seventeen.
Chuck: So, did you go to college right away?
Melissa: No, because my English wasn't very good. I studied English for two years first.
Chuck: Wow, your English is really fluent now.
Melissa: Thanks. Your English is pretty good, too.
Chuck: Yeah, but I was born here.

3 YEARS 🔲

1 Listen and practice.

1215 (twelve fifteen)   1769 (seventeen sixty-nine)   1812 (eighteen twelve)

1906 (nineteen oh six)   1917 (nineteen seventeen)   1949 (nineteen forty-nine)

2 Look at the pictures of Melissa and answer the questions.

a) When was Melissa born?
b) When did she start school?
c) When did she come to the U.S.?
d) When did she enter college?

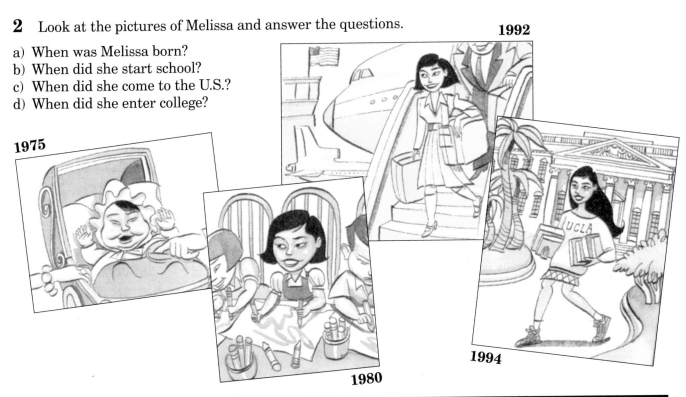

4 LISTENING 🔲

Where were these people born? When were they born? Listen
and complete the chart.

	Elizabeth Taylor	Michael J. Fox	Mel Gibson
Place of birth	....	....	....
Year of birth	....	....	....

5 GRAMMAR FOCUS: Statements and questions with *was* and *were* 🔲

I	**was**	born in Korea.
He	**wasn't**	
She		

You	**were**	born in the U.S.
We	**weren't**	
They		

When **were** you born?
  I **was** born in 1975.

Were you born in the U.S.?
  No, I **wasn't**.

Were your parents born in Korea?
  Yes, they **were**.

wasn't = was not
weren't = were not

1   Complete the conversations.

A: Where _were_ you born?
B: I .... born in Brazil.
A: .... your parents born there, too?
B: Yes, they .... They .... born in Rio.

A: When .... your daughter born?
B: She .... born in 1990.
A: How old .... you then?
B: I .... twenty-five.

A: How .... your weekend?
B: It .... OK.
A: .... the weather nice?
B: No, it .... It rained every day.

2   *Pair work*   Complete the questions with **was** or **were**.
Then ask and answer questions with a partner.

a) .... you born in this city?
b) When .... you born?
c) .... your parents born here?
d) When .... your mother born?
e) When .... your father born?
f) .... you a good student in high school?
g) What .... your favorite subject?
h) .... you good at sports?
i) .... you good at languages?
j) Who .... your first English teacher?

A: Were you born in this city?
B: No, I wasn't. I was born in Hong Kong.

CENTRAL HIGH SCHOOL
Unified School District

NAME: Gordon, Megan   YEAR: SENIOR
ACADEMIC YEAR: 1993-94

CLASS	TEACHER	GRADE
ENGLISH	Ms. MacLean	A
CALCULUS	Mr. Walton	B
SPANISH	Mrs. Myer	A
PHYSICAL EDUCATION	Mr. Renzi	B
GERMAN	Miss Hoffman	B
HISTORY	Mr. Armstrong	A
CHEMISTRY	Ms. Clayton	C

6 PRONUNCIATION: Negative contractions 📼

1 Listen and practice.

one syllable	*two syllables*
aren't	isn't
weren't	wasn't
don't	doesn't
	didn't

2 Practice these sentences.
I **didn't** see them because they **weren't** there.
He **isn't** here because he **wasn't** well.
She **doesn't** know that we **aren't** home.

7 CONVERSATION 📼

Listen and practice.

Melissa: How about you, Chuck?
 Where did you grow up?
Chuck: Well, I was born in Ohio,
 but I grew up in Texas.
Melissa: And when did you come to
 Los Angeles?
Chuck: In 1978. I went to college here.
Melissa: Oh. What was your major?
Chuck: Drama. I was an actor for
 five years after college.
Melissa: That's interesting. So why did you
 become a hairdresser?
Chuck: Because I needed the money. And
 because I was good at it. Look.
 What do you think?

8 GRAMMAR FOCUS: Wh-questions with *did*, *was*, and *were* 🔲

Where did you grow up?	I grew up **in Texas**.
Why did you become a hairdresser?	I became a hairdresser **because I needed the money**.
When did you come to Los Angeles?	I came to L.A. **in 1978**.
How old were you in 1978?	I was **eighteen**.
What was your major in college?	It was **drama**.
Who was your first friend in L.A.?	My first friend was **Bob Rivers**.
How was your vacation?	It was **great**.

What's the question?   Look at these responses. What are the questions?

When were you born?

a) I was born in 1975.

c) I grew up in Los Angeles.

b) I was born in Mexico City.

d) I went to high school in Los Angeles.

f) My favorite course in high school was calculus.

e) My best friend in high school was John Park.

g) I was eighteen years old when I entered college.

i) I chose history because it was interesting.

h) My major in college was history.

▶ **Interchange 15: Timeline**

Turn to page IC-20 to make a timeline of the important events in your life.

9 READING 🔛

1 Read about these people in the paragraphs below. Match the people with the paragraphs.

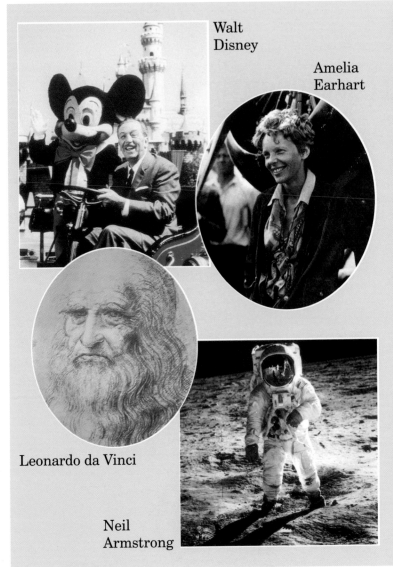

Walt
Disney

Amelia
Earhart

Leonardo da Vinci

Neil
Armstrong

Some famous people

.... This Italian painter lived from 1452 to 1519. In about 1504 he painted the *Mona Lisa*, the most famous painting in the world. The *Mona Lisa* is now in the Louvre Museum in Paris. It was stolen in 1911, but it was found again two years later.

.... In 1928 this aviator became the first woman to fly across the Atlantic Ocean as a passenger. In 1932 she completed a solo transatlantic flight. She also tried to fly around the world, but she disappeared over the Pacific in 1937.

.... This artist and film producer was the creator of Mickey Mouse. Mickey Mouse's first animated cartoon appeared in 1928. Mickey Mouse soon became the world's most popular animated cartoon character, and he received over 2,000 letters a day.

.... This astronaut was the first human to walk on the moon. He stepped onto the moon on July 20, 1969. He said, "That's one small step for man, one giant leap for mankind."

2 Complete the chart.

Name	Profession	One important thing he or she did	Date
Walt Disney	....	....	....
....	....	....	....
....	....	....	....
....	....	....	....

3 Write a few sentences about a famous person from your country.

16 Hello. Is Jennifer there, please?

1 SNAPSHOT

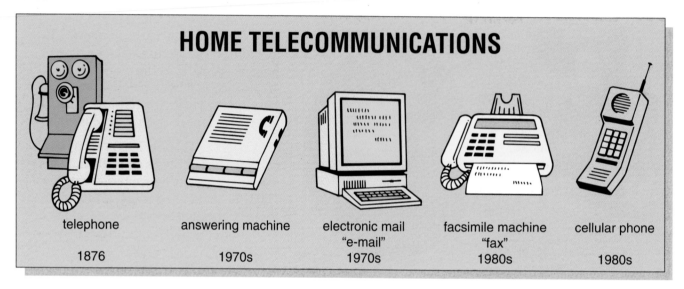

HOME TELECOMMUNICATIONS

telephone	answering machine	electronic mail "e-mail"	facsimile machine "fax"	cellular phone
1876	1970s	1970s	1980s	1980s

What telecommunications equipment do you have at home? ....
What equipment do you want? ....

2 CONVERSATION 🔲

1 Listen and practice.

Tracy: Hello?

Michael: Hi, Tracy. This is Michael. Is Jennifer there?

Tracy: I'm sorry, Michael, she's at her parents' house. She's having dinner with them. Do you want to leave her a message?

Michael: Oh, I'm not sure. It's a little complicated.

Tracy: I have an idea. I'm going out now. So call again and leave her a message on the machine.

Michael: That's a good idea.

Tracy: And don't worry, I'm not going to listen to it.

Michael: Thanks, Tracy. You're a real pal.

2 Now listen to Michael's message. Why did he call Jennifer?

3 PLACES 📼

1 Listen and practice.

Jennifer isn't here right now . . .

She's **at** work.
   at class.
   at the pool.
   at her parents' house.
   at the office.
   at the mall.

She's **in** South America.
   in the hospital.

She's **on** vacation.
   on a trip.

at the mall

Jennifer can't come to the phone right now . . .

She's **in** bed.   She's **on** the roof.
   in the shower.

on the roof

2 *Pair work* Make a telephone call and ask for one of the people below. Your partner tells you where the person is.

A: Hello, is .... there, please?
B: I'm sorry, he can't come to the phone right now. He's . . .
   (She's not here right now. She's . . .)

Michael

Brian

Victor

Lisa

Sarah

Nicole

4 GRAMMAR FOCUS: Subject and object pronouns 🔊

	me		I	
	you		you	
They left	her	a message, but	she	didn't get it.
	him		he	
	us		we	
	them		they	

Pair work   Complete these telephone conversations with pronouns.
Then practice with a partner.

A: Is Robert there, please?
B: .... 'm sorry, ... 's not here right now.
   Do .... want to leave .... a message?
A: Yes, this is David. Please tell .... to call .... at work.
B: Can .... tell .... your phone number there?
A: Sure, ... 's 555-2981.

A: Can .... speak with Mr. Ford, please?
B: .... 's not in today. But maybe .... can help ....
A: Can .... tell .... to call John Rivers?
B: John Rivers. OK. Does .... have your number?
A: Yes, ... 'm sure he has ....

A: This is the answering machine for Tom and Bill.
   Please leave .... a message after the tone.
B: Bill, this is Maria. .... left your hat and gloves here yesterday.
   If .... need .... , come and pick .... up this evening.
   Hey, ... love your hat. Where did you buy .... ?

5 CONVERSATION 🔊

Listen and practice.

Michael: Hello?
Jennifer: Hello, Michael. This is Jennifer.
          I got your message.
Michael: Great. So, do you want to go to
          the movies on Thursday?
Jennifer: I'm really sorry, but I can't.
          I have to stay home and study.
Michael: That's too bad.
Jennifer: You know, I'm having a little
          party next Saturday. Do you
          want to come?
Michael: That sounds great. What time
          does it start?
Jennifer: Around eight o'clock.
Michael: OK. See you then.

6 GRAMMAR FOCUS: Verb + *to* + verb 🔲

Do you **want to go** to the movies?
   I **want to go** to the movies.
   I don't **want to stay** home.
	Do you **have to stay** home?
	   I **have to stay** home on Thursday.
	   I **need to study**.
		Do you **like to go** to parties?
		   Of course I **like to go** to parties.

1 Complete these conversations with **have to**, **need to**, **like to**, or **want to**. Then practice with a partner.

A: This is a beautiful hat. I .... buy it.
B: Please don't buy it. We .... save money.

A: I love Chinese, and I .... speak it fluently.
B: Then you .... study very hard. It's a difficult language.

A: Do you .... go dancing tonight?
B: I really .... go, but I can't. I .... work late.

A: I .... work this Saturday, so let's go to the beach.
B: That sounds great. But we .... clean the house first.

A: Do you .... go to a party next Friday?
B: Thanks, but I don't .... go to parties.

2 *Pair work* Write answers to these questions. Then compare with a partner.

a) What are three things you have to do this week?
b) What are three things you need to buy this month?
c) What are three things you like to do on the weekend?
d) What are three things you want to learn this year?

Drawing by Eric Teitelbaum; © 1994 The New Yorker Magazine, Inc.

7 PRONUNCIATION: *want to, have to* 🔲

1 Listen and practice. Notice the pronunciation of **want to** and **have to**.

/wanə/
I **want to** see a movie.
I **want to** go home.

/hæftə/
I **have to** meet a friend.
I **have to** work late.

2 *Pair work* Practice the conversations in exercise 1 of the Grammar Focus again. Pay attention to **want to** and **have to**.

8 EXCUSES

1 *Pair work*   How often do you use these excuses? Check **often**, **sometimes**, or **never**. What are your three favorite excuses? Compare with a partner.

	often	sometimes	never
I have to work late.	☐	☐	☐
I have to study.	☐	☐	☐
I have to go to bed early.	☐	☐	☐
I have to save money.	☐	☐	☐
I'm going to visit my parents.	☐	☐	☐
I'm going to go to a lecture.	☐	☐	☐
I have a terrible headache.	☐	☐	☐
I have a terrible backache.	☐	☐	☐
I want to stay home and watch television.	☐	☐	☐
I want to stay home and read.	☐	☐	☐

2 *Class activity*   Write down three places you want to go this weekend. Choose a specific day and time. Then invite classmates to go with you.

A: Do you want to .... on .... ?
B: I'm sorry, but I can't. I have to ....
A: Do you want to .... on .... ?
B: That sounds great. When do you want to meet?

▶**Interchange 16:
Let's make a date**
Student A turns to page IC-19 and Student B turns to page IC-21. Check your calendar and make a date!

9 LISTENING ▭

1   Jennifer invited friends to a party on Saturday. Listen to the messages on her answering machine. Who can come? Who can't come?

	can come	can't come
Kumiko	☐	☐
David	☐	☐
Sarah	☐	☐
Victor	☐	☐
Nicole	☐	☐

2   Listen again. For those who can't come, what reason do they give?

name	reason
....	....
....	....

10 READING 🔳

FREE ACTIVITIES THIS WEEKEND

CITY MUSEUM TRAVEL SERIES

If you want to travel, but don't have enough money, see movies on Japan, Indonesia, Brazil, Italy, and Australia. Saturday and Sunday at 2:30 P.M. There are only 100 seats in the theater, so come early.

CANINE CLUB SHOW

County Fairgrounds, Saturday at 2:00 P.M. 100 dogs of all shapes and sizes show their talents. Come and vote for the best dog. No cats, please. Sandwiches and soda sold at the show.

ROCK CONCERT AT UNIVERSITY PARK

Do you want to hear some great music? Five student bands are going to play at University Park Saturday evening from 9:00 P.M. to midnight. Bring your own food and drink.

LIBRARY LECTURE SERIES

"How to find the job you really want."

Two-hour lecture. Advice on choosing and getting the right job for you. City Library Auditorium, Saturday at 10:00 A.M. Coffee and rolls provided.

SUMMER FASHION SHOW

Golden Shopping Plaza, Sunday at 3:00 P.M. Men's and women's swimwear and summer wear. See 25 fabulous models in the latest fashions. All clothing on sale after the show for under $50.

CRAFTS FAIR

Need to buy a present for your mother, husband, or boss? Come to a crafts fair in front of City Hall on Sunday from 9:00 A.M. to 5:00 P.M. Find pottery, jewelry, paintings, sculpture, etc., and food from around the world.

1 Read the article. Then write down two activities where you can . . .

a) buy clothes or jewelry ....   c) sit indoors ....
b) buy food ....   d) be outdoors ....

2 *Pair work* List three things you want to do. Then compare with a partner. Find one activity you can do together.

First choice: ....
Second choice: ....
Third choice: ....

Review of Units 13–16

1 Classroom rules

Write down four things you have to do in class.
Write down four things you can't do in class.
Compare with a partner.

You have to listen to the teacher . . .
You can't smoke . . .

2 Locations

1 Pair work Take turns giving the location of these places. Give the location in two different ways.

a) parking lot
b) drugstore
c) night club
d) bus stop
e) public restroom

A: The parking lot is on Second Avenue.
B: The parking lot is across from the Korean restaurant.

2 Pair work Give directions to two different places on the map.
Your partner guesses the destination.

A: Walk up First Avenue and turn left. It's on the right, on the corner of First and Lincoln.
B: It's the Japanese restaurant.
A: Right.

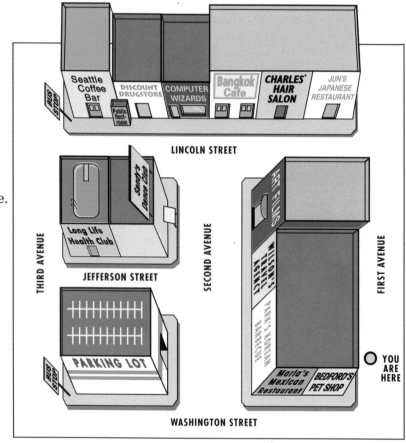

3 No, she wasn't!

1 Class activity Write three false statements about famous people in the past. Read your sentences to the class. Can anyone correct them?

Marilyn Monroe was a famous tennis player.
Elvis Presley . . .

A: Marilyn Monroe was a famous tennis player.
B: No, she wasn't. She was a movie star.

4 Tell us about it

Group work   Tell your classmates some of the things you did
last week. Each student then asks one question about it.

Tell them about . . .

a) something you did last week that you liked.
b) something you did last week that you didn't like.
c) someone interesting who you talked to last week.
d) something interesting that you bought last week.

A: I saw a movie last week.
B: What was the name of the movie? . . .
C: Who was in it? . . .
D: How did you like it? . . .

5 Listening ▭

Listen and choose the correct response.

a) ☐ No, they weren't.
   ☐ No, they aren't.

b) ☐ At eleven o'clock.
   ☐ No, I didn't.

c) ☐ We took the bus.
   ☐ Amy and Katherine.

d) ☐ It was great.
   ☐ Sue and Tom were.

e) ☐ I'm going to visit my parents on Sunday.
   ☐ Because I had a terrible headache.

f) ☐ I'm sorry, but I can't. I have to work.
   ☐ No, I didn't go. I was at work.

g) ☐ I'm sorry, he's not here right now.
   ☐ Stephanie is at work right now.

h) ☐ There's a restaurant on Grant Street.
   ☐ No, there isn't. Sorry.

6 Future plans

Make a list of five things you want to do in the
next five years. Then compare with a partner.

> I want to find a wife (husband).
> I want to get a job in a bank.

Interchange Activities

Directory Assistance – STUDENT A

Role play

1 You need the telephone numbers of these people. Student B is the telephone operator. You are the customer. Follow the conversation:

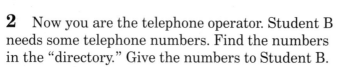

	number
Ms. Kumiko Roku	....
Ms. Ada Rodrigues	....
Mr. Marc Rudolph	....
Mr. Paul Rosen	....

Operator: Directory Assistance.
Customer: I need the number of ....
Operator: How do you spell the last name?
Customer: ....
Operator: And the first name?
Customer: ....
Operator: Thank you. The number is ....

2 Now you are the telephone operator. Student B needs some telephone numbers. Find the numbers in the "directory." Give the numbers to Student B.

DIRECTORY

375

CAPUTO, Anthony	555-4667	CHANG, Ming Li	555-0215
CAPUTO, Frank	555-9873	CHRISTIE, Robert	555-9807
CARDENA, Rafael	555-8614	CHRISTO, Rolf	555-7546
CARDENAS, Ramon	555-8654	COHEN, Andrea	555-4089
CHANG, Min Li	555-0396	COHN, Andrew	555-2390

Interchange 2   Find the differences

1 *Pair work*   How are the two pictures different? Ask questions
to find the differences.

A: Where are the sunglasses?
B: In picture A, they're on . . .
A: In picture B, they're . . .

2 *Class activity*   Talk about the differences with your classmates.

"In picture A, the sunglasses are on . . . . In picture B, they're . . ."

Interchange 1 | Directory Assistance – STUDENT B

Role play

1 You are the telephone operator. Student A is the customer. Student A needs some telephone numbers. Find the numbers in the "directory." Follow this conversation:

Operator: Directory Assistance.
Customer: I need the number of ....
Operator: How do you spell the last name?
Customer: ....
Operator: And the first name?
Customer: ....
Operator: Thank you. The number is ....

DIRECTORY	1180
ROCHE, Annette	555-8125
RODRIGUES, Ada	555-9012
RODRIGUEZ, Ana	555-6734
ROKU, Kumiko	555-1392
ROSE, Pearl	555-2516
ROSEN, Paul	555-3519
RUDOLF, Karl	555-3418
RUDOLPH, Marc	555-0926
RUSSO, Antonio	555-6775

2 Now you are the customer and Student A is the telephone operator. Ask for the numbers of these people:

	number
Ms. Min Li Chang	....
Mr. Rolf Christo	....
Miss Andrea Cohen	....
Mr. Rafael Cardena	....

Interchange 4 | What's the weather like?

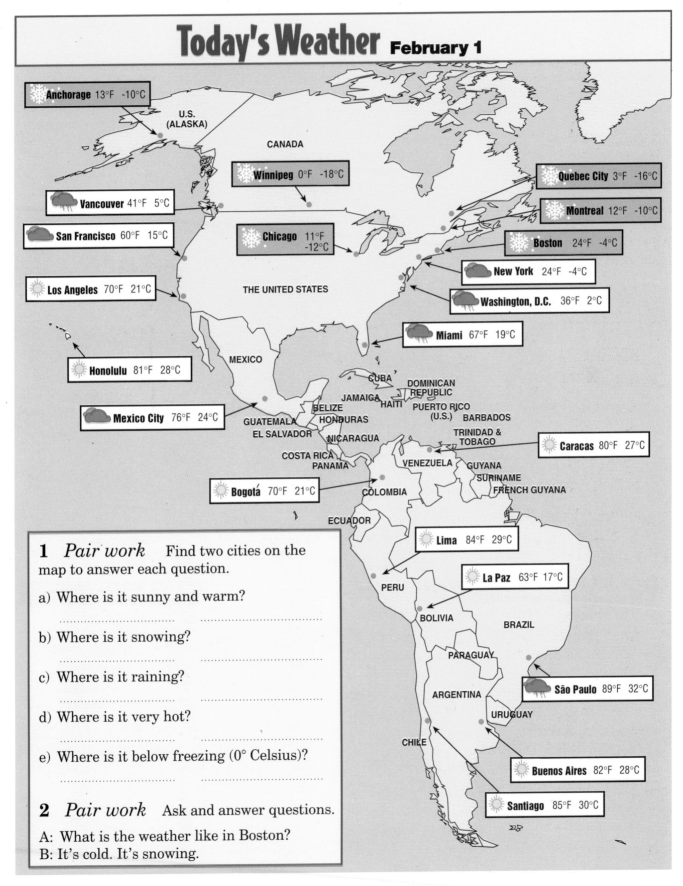

Today's Weather February 1

Anchorage 13°F -10°C

U.S. (ALASKA)

CANADA

Winnipeg 0°F -18°C

Quebec City 3°F -16°C

Vancouver 41°F 5°C

Montreal 12°F -10°C

San Francisco 60°F 15°C

Chicago 11°F -12°C

Boston 24°F -4°C

New York 24°F -4°C

THE UNITED STATES

Los Angeles 70°F 21°C

Washington, D.C. 36°F 2°C

Miami 67°F 19°C

Honolulu 81°F 28°C

MEXICO

CUBA

DOMINICAN REPUBLIC

JAMAICA HAITI

PUERTO RICO (U.S.)

BARBADOS

Mexico City 76°F 24°C

BELIZE

GUATEMALA HONDURAS

EL SALVADOR

NICARAGUA

TRINIDAD & TOBAGO

Caracas 80°F 27°C

COSTA RICA

PANAMA

VENEZUELA

GUYANA

SURINAME

FRENCH GUYANA

Bogotá 70°F 21°C

COLOMBIA

ECUADOR

Lima 84°F 29°C

PERU

La Paz 63°F 17°C

BOLIVIA

BRAZIL

PARAGUAY

São Paulo 89°F 32°C

ARGENTINA

URUGUAY

CHILE

Buenos Aires 82°F 28°C

Santiago 85°F 30°C

1 *Pair work*   Find two cities on the map to answer each question.

a) Where is it sunny and warm?

....

b) Where is it snowing?

....

c) Where is it raining?

....

d) Where is it very hot?

....

e) Where is it below freezing (0° Celsius)?

....

2 *Pair work*   Ask and answer questions.

A: What is the weather like in Boston?
B: It's cold. It's snowing.

Interchange 3 Geography quiz

1 *Pair work* Work with a partner to find the answers.

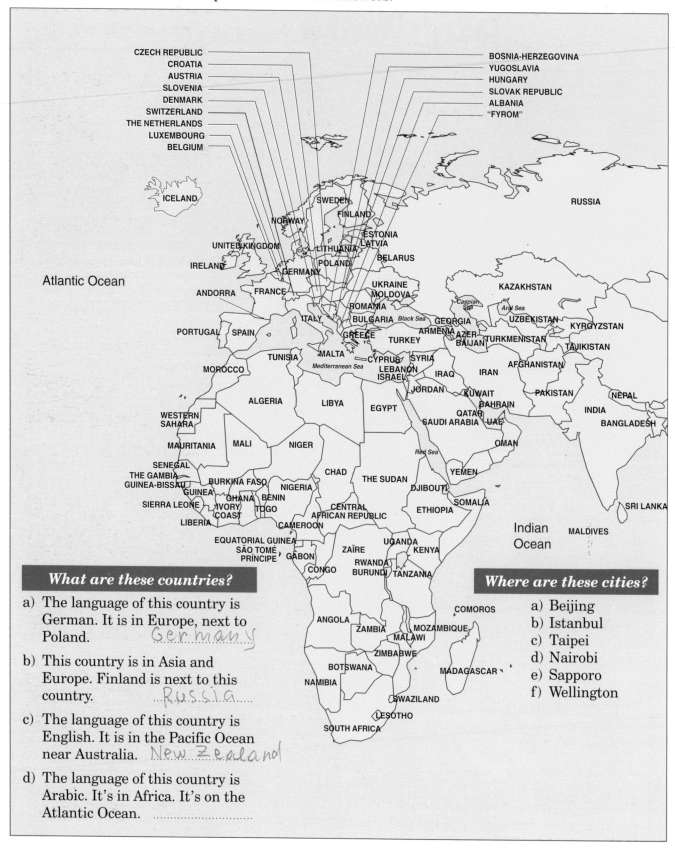

What are these countries?

a) The language of this country is German. It is in Europe, next to Poland. *Germany*

b) This country is in Asia and Europe. Finland is next to this country. *Russia*

c) The language of this country is English. It is in the Pacific Ocean near Australia. *New Zealand*

d) The language of this country is Arabic. It's in Africa. It's on the Atlantic Ocean. ....

Where are these cities?

a) Beijing

b) Istanbul

c) Taipei

d) Nairobi

e) Sapporo

f) Wellington

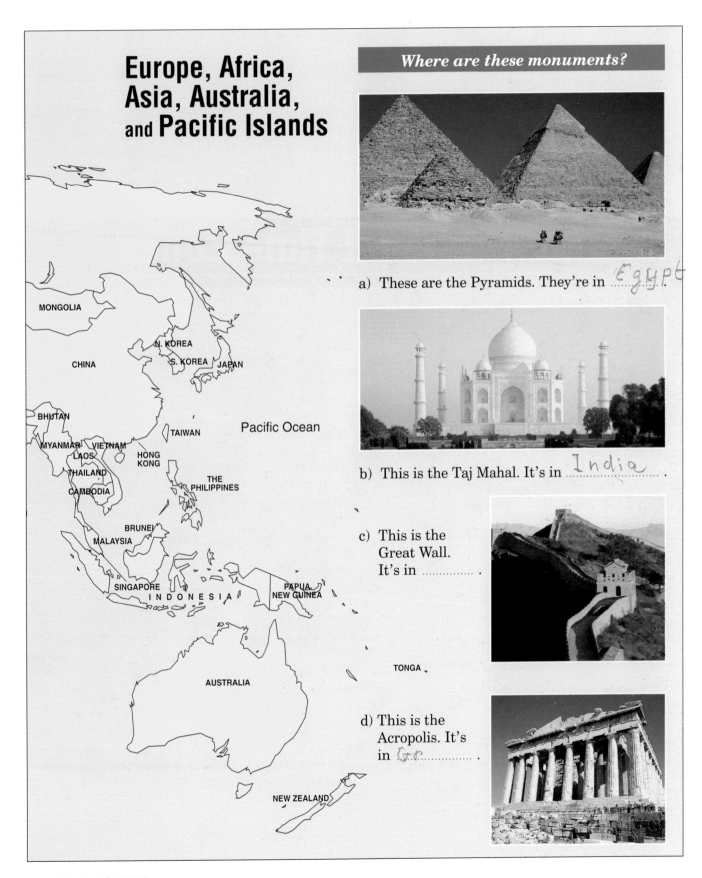

Europe, Africa, Asia, Australia, and Pacific Islands

MONGOLIA

N. KOREA
S. KOREA
JAPAN
CHINA

BHUTAN
TAIWAN
Pacific Ocean
MYANMAR VIETNAM
LAOS
HONG
KONG
THAILAND
THE
PHILIPPINES
CAMBODIA

BRUNEI
MALAYSIA

SINGAPORE
I N D O N E S I A
PAPUA
NEW GUINEA

TONGA

AUSTRALIA

NEW ZEALAND

Where are these monuments?

a) These are the Pyramids. They're in ....Egypt.

b) This is the Taj Mahal. It's in ....India.....

c) This is the Great Wall. It's in ....

d) This is the Acropolis. It's in Gr............. .

2 *Group work*   Compare your answers with another pair.

Interchange 5 Time zones

Pair work   Ask and answer questions about the cities below. Use expressions from the box.

A: What time is it in Los Angeles?
B: It's 4:00 A.M. (It's four o'clock in the morning.)
A: What are people doing?
B: They're sleeping.

sleeping	working	having dinner
getting up	having lunch	watching
getting dressed	going home	television
going to work	shopping	

International Time Zones

A B C D E F G H I J K L M N O P Q R S T U V W X

1:00 AM 2:00 AM 3:00 AM 4:00 AM 5:00 AM 6:00 AM 7:00 AM 8:00 AM 9:00 AM 10:00 AM 11:00 AM 12:00 PM 1:00 PM 2:00 PM 3:00 PM 4:00 PM 5:00 PM 6:00 PM 7:00 PM 8:00 PM 9:00 PM 10:00 PM 11:00 PM 12:00 AM

Interchange 6 Class survey

1 *Class activity* Find at least one person in the class who does these things.

A: Do you get up at 5:00 A.M.?
B: No, I don't get up at 5:00 A.M.
  I get up at 7:00 A.M.

A: Do you get up at 5:00 A.M.?
C: Yes, I get up at 5:00 A.M. every day.

2 *Class activity*
Tell the class about the
students you talk to.

A: Juan and Keiko work at night.
B: Celia works at night, too.

Find someone who . . .

	Name
. . . gets up at 5:00 A.M. on weekdays.	
. . . gets up at noon on Saturdays.	
. . . doesn't eat breakfast.	
. . has breakfast in bed.	
. . . works at night.	
. . . works on the weekend.	
. . . lives downtown.	
. . . lives in the country.	
. . . lives alone.	
. . . rides a bicycle to class.	
. . . rides a motorcycle to class.	
. . . walks to class.	
. . . watches television every day.	
. . . doesn't have a television.	
. . . wears blue jeans every day.	
. . . speaks three languages.	

riding a motorcycle to class

having breakfast in bed

Interchange 7 | **Find the differences**

Pair work   Write down five differences between Bill's apartment
and Jane's apartment. Then compare with your partner.

Jane's Apartment

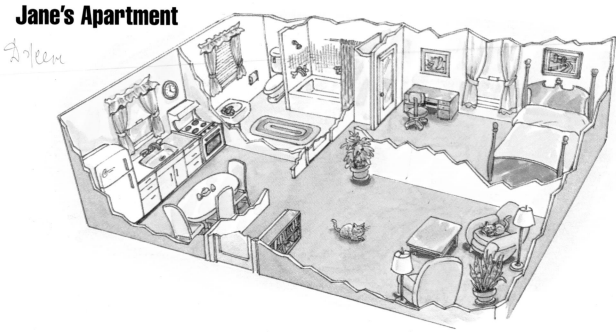

Bill's Apartment

There are four chairs in Bill's kitchen. There are three chairs in Jane's kitchen.
There's a sofa in Bill's living room, but there's no sofa in Jane's living room.

....

....

....

....

....

Interchange 8 | The perfect job

1 *Pair work* You're looking for a job. Which of these things do you want in a job? Answer the questions. Then ask your partner the same questions.

Job Survey

Do you want to . . .	Me Yes	No	My partner Yes	No
a) talk to people?	☐	☐	☐	☐
b) help people?	☐	☐	☐	☐
c) perform in front of people?	☐	☐	☐	☐
d) work from 9 to 5?	☐	☐	☐	☐
e) make your own schedule?	☐	☐	☐	☐
f) use a computer?	☐	☐	☐	☐
g) use the telephone?	☐	☐	☐	☐
h) work outdoors?	☐	☐	☐	☐
i) work in an office?	☐	☐	☐	☐
j) have a private office?	☐	☐	☐	☐
k) work at home?	☐	☐	☐	☐
l) travel?	☐	☐	☐	☐
m) have a high salary?	☐	☐	☐	☐
n) speak English?	☐	☐	☐	☐
o) wear a uniform?	☐	☐	☐	☐
p) wear a suit?	☐	☐	☐	☐
q) wear blue jeans?	☐	☐	☐	☐

working from 9 to 5

working outdoors

2 *Class activity* Think of a good job for yourself. Then tell the class.

"I want to be a musician, because I want to . . ."

. . . work at home.

. . . perform in front of people.

. . . travel.

Interchange 9 Planning a picnic

1 *Group work* Plan a picnic with some friends.
First, find out what foods people like and don't like to eat.
Complete the chart.

Name				
Three favorite picnic foods	....	....	....	....
Favorite drink	....	....	....	....
Favorite dessert	....	....	....	....
Foods or drink he/she doesn't like	....	....	....	....

2   Now make a menu for the picnic. Choose three foods,
two drinks, and one dessert.

```
        Picnic menu

......................................
......................................
......................................
......................................
......................................
......................................
......................................
......................................
```

3 *Class activity* Compare
menus with the rest of the class.

Interchange 10 | **Hidden talents**

1 *Class activity*   Walk around the class asking questions to fill in the chart below. Find one person who **can** and one person who **can't** do each thing.

A: Can you touch your toes?
B: Yes I can. (No, I can't.)

Can you . . .	*can* (name)	*can't* (name)
1. touch your toes?	....	....
2. play a musical instrument?	....	....
3. dance the tango?	....	....
4. say "Hello" in 5 different languages?	....	....
5. swim underwater?	....	....
6. remember lots of telephone numbers?	....	....
7. write with both hands?	....	....
8. sing a song in English?	....	....
9. ride a horse?	....	....
10. juggle?	....	....
11. make your own clothes?	....	....
12. do magic tricks?	....	....

riding a horse

juggling

doing magic tricks

2   Report your results to the class.

Noriko can't touch her toes, but she knows how to juggle.

Interchange 11 | Vacation plans

1 *Pair work*   Answer questions about vacation plans, or talk
about your "dream" vacation. Then ask about your partner's plans.

	Me	*My partner*
1. When is your next vacation?	....	....
2. How long are you going to be on vacation?	....	....

April
August
July
December

for two weeks
for one week
for a long weekend
for one month

3. Where are you going to go?
4. What are you going to do?

5. How are you going to go?
6. Who are you going to go with?

7. What are you going to eat?
8. What are you going to bring back?

GUIDE BOOK

2 *Group work*   Two pairs form a group. Tell the group your
partner's plans.

"Maria's next vacation is in July. She's going to be on vacation for one week . . ."

Interchange 12 **Helpful advice**

1 *Pair work*   Look at the problems below. Give advice to each person.

> I want to lose a little weight, but I really like desserts. Ice cream is my favorite food!

> My job is very stressful. I usually work 10 hours a day and on weekends. I have backaches and headaches almost every day.

> I can never get up on time in the morning. I'm always late for work. I guess I'm not a morning person.

> I'm new in town and I don't know any people here. I want to make some friends.

2 *Class activity*   Write down two problems that you have. Then tell the class. Your classmates give you advice.

I can't sleep at night . .

A: I can't sleep at night.
B: Get up and do some work.
C: Don't drink coffee in the evening.

Interchange 13 Directions – STUDENT A

Pair work

1 Look at the map. You are on Third Avenue between Maple and Oak Streets. Ask your partner for directions to:

a) a car wash   b) a supermarket   c) a flower shop

Mark the location on the map.

A: Excuse me. Is there a car wash near here?
B: Yes, there is. It's . . .

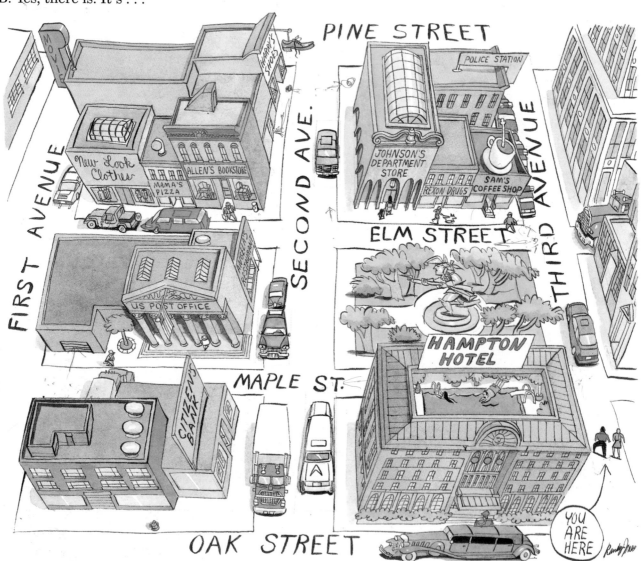

2 Now your partner asks you for directions to three places. Give your partner directions, using the expressions in the box.

Useful expressions		
Go right/left . . .	It's on the corner of . . . Street and . . . Avenue	It's next to . . .
Walk one block . . .	It's between . . . and . . .	It's behind . . .
Turn right/left . . .	It's across from . . .	It's in front of . . .

Interchange 14 | Past and present

1 *Pair work* Ask a partner questions about the past and about the present. Write down the answers.

A: As a child, did you clean your room?
B: Yes, I did. (No, I didn't.)
A: Do you clean your room now?
B: Yes I do. (No, I don't.)

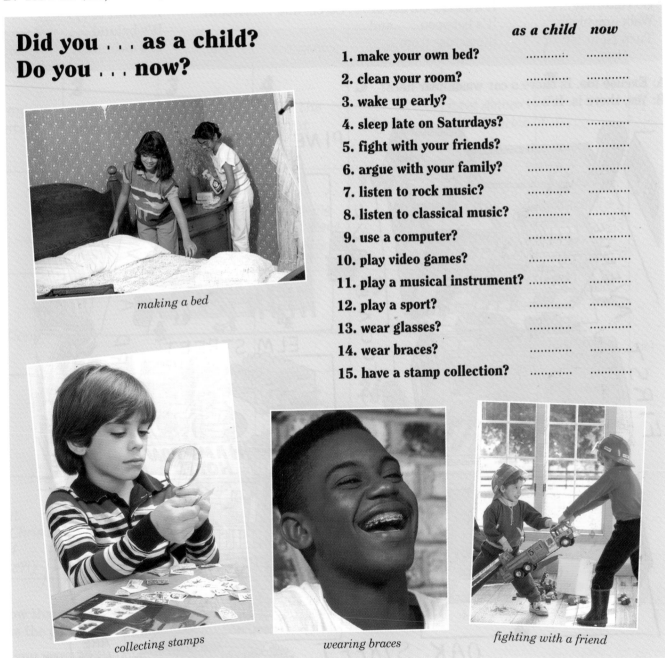

Did you . . . as a child?
Do you . . . now?

	as a child	*now*
1. make your own bed?	…………	…………
2. clean your room?	…………	…………
3. wake up early?	…………	…………
4. sleep late on Saturdays?	…………	…………
5. fight with your friends?	…………	…………
6. argue with your family?	…………	…………
7. listen to rock music?	…………	…………
8. listen to classical music?	…………	…………
9. use a computer?	…………	…………
10. play video games?	…………	…………
11. play a musical instrument?	…………	…………
12. play a sport?	…………	…………
13. wear glasses?	…………	…………
14. wear braces?	…………	…………
15. have a stamp collection?	…………	…………

making a bed

collecting stamps

wearing braces

fighting with a friend

2 *Group work* Join with another pair. Tell them about your partner.

"Tai-lin didn't clean his room as a child, but he does now."

Key Vocabulary

Unit 1 Hello. My name is Jennifer Wan.

NOUNS

Classroom items

board [bɔːd]
book
cassette player
chair
desk
dictionary
envelope [enviloup]
eraser
map
notebook
pencil
piece of paper
table
wastebasket
workbook

Other nouns

boy
class
country
English
girl
math
name
number
telephone number
umbrella
word

VERBS

am
are
is
close
find
go
open
say
see
spell
take out
write

ADVERBS

here
there
over there

PREPOSITIONS

in
on
to

PRONOUNS AND CONTRACTIONS

I	I'm
you	you're
he	he's
she	she's
it	it's

ARTICLES

a
an
the

WH-WORD

what

EXPRESSIONS

Excuse me.
What's your name?
My name is . . .
This is . . .
(It's) nice to meet you.
By the way . . .
How do you spell . . . ?
I'm sorry.
I think . . .
Please . . .
Thank you.
Yes. No.

Hellos

Hello./Hi.
Good morning.
Good afternoon.
Good evening.

Good-byes

Good-bye./Bye./Bye-bye.
Have a nice day.
See you tomorrow.
Good night.

ADJECTIVES

Possessives	Titles	Numbers 1–10	Other
my	Mr.	(See page 5)	first
your	Ms.		last
his	Mrs.		right
her	Miss		

Unit 2 What's this called in English?

NOUNS

Personal items

address book
book bag
briefcase
calculator
comb
eyeglass case
eyeglasses (pl)
credit card
driver's license
glasses (pl)
hairbrush
handbag
key
pen
photo
sunglasses (pl)
tissue
wallet

Other nouns

address
baby
bed
bedroom
cabinet
classroom
cushion
daughter
newspaper
question
remote control
sofa
teacher
television
thing

VERBS

carry
pick up
put
watch

ADVERBS

just
in bed
not
right there/here
tonight
very

ADJECTIVES

different
new
ready
nice

Possessives

my
your
his
her
our
their

PREPOSITIONS

behind
in
in front of
next to
on
under

PRONOUNS

everything
this/these

WH-WORD

where

EXPRESSIONS

What's this called?	Let me see.
What are these called?	Great.
This is . . .	Actually. . .
These are . . .	Maybe . . .
Thank you very much.	I know.
Thanks for watching . . .	I don't know.
Just one more question.	Well . . .

Unit 3 Where are you from?

NOUNS

Countries*
Argentina
Australia
Austria
Bolivia
Brazil
Cambodia
Canada
Chile
China
Colombia
Costa Rica
Cuba
the Dominican Republic
Ecuador
Egypt
England
France
Germany
Guatemala
Haiti
Honduras
Hungary
India
Indonesia
Ireland
Italy
Japan
Korea
Laos
Lebanon
Malaysia
Mexico
the Netherlands
Nicaragua
Nepal
New Zealand
Panama
Paraguay
Peru
the Philippines
Poland
Portugal
Russia
Spain
Sudan
Sweden
Turkey
Uruguay
the United Kingdom
the United States
Venezuela
Vietnam

*These lists do not include all countries of the world, but do list countries that are not presented in the unit.

ADJECTIVES

Nationalities*
Argentinian
Australian
Austrian
Bolivian
Brazilian
Cambodian
Canadian
Chilean
Chinese
Colombian
Costa Rican
Cuban
Dominican
Ecuadorian
Egyptian
English
French
German
Guatemalan
Haitian
Honduran
Hungarian
Indian
Indonesian
Irish
Italian
Japanese
Korean
Laotian
Lebanese
Malaysian
Mexican
Dutch
Nicaraguan
Nepalese
New Zealander
Panamanian
Paraguayan
Peruvian
Filipino
Polish
Portuguese
Russian
Spanish
Sudanese
Swedish
Turkish
Uruguayan
British
American
Venezuelan
Vietnamese

NOUNS

Regions
Africa
Asia
the Caribbean
Central America
Europe
North America
South America
the Pacific

Other nouns
city
country
family
geography
immigrant
language

Languages
(See page 18.)

ADJECTIVES
good
interesting
native
official
whole

VERBS
aren't
isn't

ADVERBS
originally
very
now

PREPOSITIONS
from
of
in (Spanish)

EXPRESSIONS
Really?
Oh.
Oh, right.
Where are you from?
I'm from . . .
Here. Take it.
So . . .

Unit 4 Clothes and weather

NOUNS

Clothes
bathing suit
blouse
blue jeans
boots
coat
dress
hat
high heels
pajamas
running shoes
scarf
shirt
shoes
shorts
skirt
slacks
suit
tennis shoes
tie (necktie)
T-shirt
watch (wristwatch)

Seasons
spring
summer
fall
winter

Other nouns
degree
taxi
temperature
weather

ADJECTIVES

Colors
beige
black
blue
brown
gray
green
orange
pink
purple
red
white
yellow

Weather
cloudy
cold
cool
hot
humid
sunny
warm
windy

Other adjectives
dark
light
Celsius
Fahrenheit

Numbers 11–100
(See page 25.)

VERBS
drive
play (tennis)
rain
run
snow
swim
take (a taxi)
take (a walk)
walk
wear

ADVERBS
really
today

PREPOSITION
below (zero)

CONJUNCTIONS
and
but
so

WH-WORD
What color

EXPRESSIONS
Uh-oh.
What's the matter?
Great idea.
Come on!
Let's . . .
What color . . . ?
What's the weather like?

Unit 5 What are you doing?

NOUNS	VERBS	ADVERBS	PREPOSITIONS
Meals	attend	*Times*	after
breakfast	call	at night	at
lunch	clean (the house)	in the afternoon	to
dinner	dance	in the evening	**CONJUNCTION**
Other nouns	get dressed	in the morning	if
clock	get up	on Saturday	**WH-WORDS**
coffee	have breakfast,	this month	what time
conference	lunch, dinner	this week	who
dish	go (to the movies)	*Clock time*	why
movie	go (to work)	A.M./P.M.	
television (TV)	remember	midnight	
week	shop	noon	
work	sit	at noon	
	sleep	o'clock	
	stay (in bed)		
	vacuum		
	wash (the dishes)		
	watch (television)		
	work		

ADJECTIVE	EXPRESSIONS
awake	Hey! What time is it?
	Of course. It's . . . o'clock.
	See you at . . . It's a quarter after/to . . .
	That's OK. It's . . . minutes after/to . . .
	I'm calling from . . . . . . right?
	(Do you) remember?

Unit 6 How do you go to work?

NOUNS		VERBS	ADVERBS	ADJECTIVES
Days of the week	*Places*	come	*Places*	alone
Sunday	apartment	do (work)	downtown	big
Monday	city	get (=pick up)	home	lucky
Tuesday	country	go	in the city	public
Wednesday	house	have (a ride)	in the country	retired
Thursday	park	hope	in the suburbs	**PREPOSITIONS**
Friday	restaurant	leave (for)	*Times*	like
Saturday	school	live	early	near
Family	suburbs	meet	every day	with
brother	*Transportation*	need	every morning	**PRONOUNS**
child	bus	read	late	both
children (*pl*)	car	serve	on Sundays	me
daughter	ferry	sleep in	on Mondays	us
father	subway	speak	all day	**WH-WORD**
husband	tow truck	take (a break)	not too early	how
mother	train	take (the bus,	at (nine) o'clock	**EXPRESSIONS**
parent	*Other nouns*	subway)	at midnight	a lot of
sister	job	use	at noon	OK.
son	people (*pl*)	wait (for)	on weekdays	Sure.
wife	ride	work (=function)	on the weekend	That's good.
	work		on weekends	What about you?
			Other adverbs	You're lucky!
			by bus, subway	
			together	
			too (not too early)	

Unit 7 Does the apartment have a view?

NOUNS

Homes/Rooms
apartment
basement
bathroom
bedroom
closet
dining room
family room
garage
house
kitchen
living room
room
swimming pool
view (of)
yard

Furniture
armchair
bed
bookcase
chair
clock
coffee table
computer
desk
dresser
lamp
microwave oven
mirror

picture
refrigerator
rug
sofa
stove
table
television

Other
help
neighbor
river
yard sale

VERBS
move in
need

ADVERBS
only
next weekend

ADJECTIVES
some
any

WH-WORDS
How many
What else

EXPRESSIONS
Guess what!
No problem.
What else . . . ?
What is . . . like?

That sounds great.
Right.
Of course.
There's . . .

There are some . . .
There's no . . .
There aren't any . . .

Unit 8 What do you do?

NOUNS

Jobs/Professions
accountant
airline pilot
air traffic controller
athlete
cashier
chef
college professor
(restaurant) cook
doctor
flight attendant
judge
lawyer

musician
nurse
police officer
receptionist
salesclerk
salesperson
security guard
singer
teacher
travel agent
waiter
waitress

Other nouns
boyfriend
computer
department store
electronics store
gun
hospital
hotel
money
office
salary
store
uniform

VERBS
agree
handle
hear
look (for)
repair
sell
sit
stand
teach
talk

ADVERBS
exactly
really
too

ADJECTIVES
boring
dangerous
difficult
easy
exciting
high
interesting

low
pleasant
relaxing
safe
stressful
unpleasant

WH-WORD
Who

EXPRESSIONS
How do you like it?
How are things with you?
Not bad.
I hear . . .
Now that's . . . !

Unit 9 I love strawberries!

NOUNS

Dairy
butter
cheese
egg(s)*
milk
yogurt
Desserts
cake
chocolate
cookie(s)
ice cream
pie (apple pie)
Drinks
lemonade
milk
soda
tea (green tea)

Fish
salmon
shrimp
Fruit
apple(s)
banana(s)
mango (mangoes)
orange(s)
strawberry
 (strawberries)
Meat
bacon
beef
chicken
hamburger (meat)
hot dog(s)
lamb

Starches
bean(s)
bread
bun(s)
pasta
potato (potatoes)
rice
Vegetables
bean(s)
broccoli
carrot(s)
celery
green bean(s)
onion(s)
pepper(s)
tomato (tomatoes)

Other foods
mayonnaise
potato salad
salad
sandwich(es)
snack(s)
toast
Other nouns
barbecue
freezer
meal
picnic

*Plurals are given here for foods that are countable nouns.

VERBS
buy
choose
drink
eat
hate
love
love to
make
need to
think
try
want

ADVERBS
always
ever
never
often
seldom
sometimes
usually

ADJECTIVES
awful
delicious
Japanese-style
same
traditional

PRONOUN
everyone

EXPRESSIONS
. . . is / are good for you.
How about some . . . ?
Let's not . . .
We need to buy . . .
I have . . . for breakfast.

Why don't you . . . ?
I love to try new things.
To make a sandwich, you need . . .

Unit 10 Can you swim very well?

NOUNS

Sports
baseball
basketball
football
golf
Ping-Pong
skating
 (ice-skating)
skiing
soccer
swimming
tennis
volleyball
team sport
individual sport

Games
board game
card game
chess
video game

Other nouns
date
girlfriend
lap (of a pool)
poetry
pool
sport

VERBS
can / can't
cook
dance
dive
draw
fix (a car)
have (a date)
know how to
play (a game)
play (a sport)
play (the piano)
sing
skate (ice-skate)
ski

ADVERBS
at all
even
fluently
quite well
too / either
(not) very well

ADJECTIVES
late
terrific

EXPRESSIONS
I can't even . . .
I can teach you how to . . .
In fact . . .
Wow!
What's that?
I know how to . . .
I'm good at . . .
There's one thing
 (that) . . .
She's not good at
 remembering things.
She's an hour late!

Unit 11 When's your birthday?

NOUNS		VERBS	ADVERBS	EXPRESSIONS
birthday	place	blow out (candles)	next week (month, year,	I hope so.
birthday cake	present	celebrate	summer, Saturday, etc.)	Nice!
candles	speech	kiss	probably	How old are you?
day	year	order	tomorrow	I'm . . . years old.
diploma		receive	tomorrow night	I bet . . .
fireworks	*Months*	shout	tonight	It's going to be fun.
friend	*(See page 68.)*			Happy Birthday!
fun				Happy New Year!
graduation				have a good time
holiday				

ADJECTIVES		WH-WORD
embarrassing	*Ordinal*	How old
next	*numbers*	
special	*(See page 68.)*	

(month, party — remaining nouns)
month
party

Unit 12 What's the matter?

NOUNS			ADJECTIVES				
Body parts	shoulder	*Other nouns*	bad	every	free	sad	terrible
arm	stomach	appointment	better	fine	heavy	sore	
back	tooth *(pl* teeth)	aspirin					
ear	*Illnesses*	bath					
eye	backache	exercise					
foot *(pl* feet)	cold	opening					
hand	earache	pill					
head	fever	place					
leg	(the) flu	(=residence)					
mouth	headache	water					
neck	sore throat						
nose	stomachache						

VERBS		ADVERBS	
feel (sad)	lose (weight)	a little	just
forget	relax	already	soon
get (exercise)	sit down	early	then
go out	take (a bath)		
lift	take (a pill)		

EXPRESSIONS

How are you?
I'm fine.
That's fine.
I'm just feeling a little sad.
I don't think so.
Listen.
Thanks a lot.
How do you feel?
What's wrong?
That's too bad.
I hope you feel better soon.
I'm sorry to hear that.

I have a headache (a stomachache, a cold, the flu, a sore throat, sore eyes, etc.).
Hello, this is . . .
Can I make an appointment?
Take these pills every four hours.
I have trouble remembering . . .
When is . . . again?
Go home.
Go to bed. / Stay in bed.

Unit 13 Can you help me, please?

NOUNS		VERBS	ADJECTIVES	EXPRESSIONS
Places	post office	get (to a place)	expensive	Can you help me, please?
bookstore	restroom	look up	far	Is there a . . . near here?
building	supermarket	turn		Is . . . far from here?
bus stop		turn around		It's right behind you.
department	*Other nouns*			Oh, no!
store	block			You're welcome.
drugstore	gasoline			How do I get to . . . ?
gas station	magazine			
hotel	stamp			
newsstand				
parking lot				

ADVERBS	PREPOSITIONS
left / right	across from
on the left / right	down
indoors / outdoors	on the corner of
right (=exactly)	up

Unit 14 Did you have a good weekend?

NOUNS	VERBS		ADJECTIVE	EXPRESSIONS
activity	exercise	sleep	tired	Sort of.
computer	give	study		Of course . . .
computer game	go dancing	take off (time)		That sounds like fun.
dance club	go shopping	tell		Yeah.
letter	go skating	visit		Did you have fun?
video	hike	wash (clothes)	PREPOSITION	We had a great time.
weekend	invite		before	
	listen (to)	*Irregular past*		
	make	*(See page 91.)*		
	miss			
	rent			

Unit 15 Where were you born?

NOUNS	VERBS	ADJECTIVES	WH-WORDS	EXPRESSIONS
actor	be born	best	when	Where were you born?
calculus	become (*past* became)	fluent	why	I was born in Korea.
college	choose (*past* chose)	pretty good		I went to college
course	enter (college)			I needed the money.
drama	get married		CONJUNCTION	Look.
(best) friend	graduate		because	What do you think?
hairdresser	grow up (*past* grew up)			
high school	happen			
major				
subject	ADVERBS		PREPOSITION	
	right away pretty		after	
	early (=quite)			

Unit 16   Hello. Is Jennifer there, please?

NOUNS		VERBS	PRONOUNS		EXPRESSIONS
Places	*Other nouns*	call	I	me	I have an idea.
beach	idea	get (a message)	you	you	Don't worry.
hospital	guitar	leave (a message)	she	her	You're a real pal.
mall	grandparent	pick up	he	him	I'm sorry, but I can't.
office	lecture	save (money)	it	it	You know, . . .
roof	(answering)	stay (home)	we	us	Around (eight o'clock).
shower	machine	have to	they	them	
yard	message	like to			*Telephone language*
	pal	need to			Is Jennifer there?
	party	want to			She isn't here right now.
	rock music				She can't come to the
	trip				phone right now.
		ADVERBS			Do you want to leave
ADJECTIVES		again			(her) a message?
complicated real		at class	PREPOSITIONS		Leave (her) a message
little sure		at home	around		on the machine.
		early	at		
		on vacation			

Acknowledgments

Text Credits

2 *The Cambridge Encyclopedia* © 1990 Cambridge University Press.
14 "The Immigrants," *Business Week,* 13 July 1992.
18 *The Cambridge Encyclopedia* © 1990 Cambridge University Press.
20 *Curious Customs: The Stories Behind 296 Popular American Rituals* by Tad Tuleja © 1987 by The Stonesong Press.
36 "New Frontiers in Commuting," *Fortune,* 13 January 1992.
51 "The Best Jobs in America," *Money,* March 1994.
61 *Profiles,* in-flight magazine by Virgin Atlantic Airlines, Summer 1993; *Panati's Extraordinary Origins of Everyday Things,* HarperCollins, 1989.
62 *(Snapshot) World Almanac and Book of Facts, 1994.*
79 *Having Our Say: The Delany Sisters' First Hundred Years,* Kodansha, 1993; "Secrets of a Long Life from Two Who Ought to Know," *The New York Times,* September 18, 1993, p. B1.
88 *(Snapshot)* Leisure Trends compilation of Gallup data.
93 Adapted from Witold Rybczynski, *Waiting for the Weekend,* Penguin Books, 1991.
95 *The 1994 Information Please Almanac*
99 *Webster's College Encyclopedia,* Prentice-Hall, 1993.

Illustrators

Randy Jones 6 *(bottom)*, 22 *(top)*, 24, 31, 33 *(bottom)*, 48, 49 *(top)*, 54, 72, 77, 86, 94, 95, 97, IC–9, IC–11, IC–13, IC–14, IC–16, IC–18
Mark Kaufman 6 *(top)*, 9 *(all)*, 11 *(all)*, 12 *(bottom)*, 28, 45, 56, 61, 80, 82, 84, IC–3
Beth McNally 12 *(middle)*, 64 *(top)*
Wally Neibart 7, 23, 26, 29, 30 *(bottom)*, 70, 75, 78, 85 *(top)*, 90, IC–10
Eva Sakmar-Sullivan 21
Bill Thomson 2, 3 *(top)*, 4, 5 *(bottom)*, 8, 16 *(bottom)*, 30 *(top)*, 36, 37, 38, 49 *(bottom)*, 58, 60, 74, 83, 89, 100, 101, 102, 104
Sam Viviano 10, 12 *(top)*, 13, 15, 16 *(top)*, 22 *(bottom)*, 27, 33 *(top)*, 34, 39, 42, 43, 44, 46, 51, 62, 63, 64 *(bottom)*, 69, 71, 76, 85 *(bottom)*, 91, 92, 107
Snapshots by Phil Scheuer

Photographic Credits

The author and publisher are grateful for permission to reproduce the following photographs.

3 *(center)* Reuters/Bettmann
17 *(top)* © 1989 Jean Kugler/FPG International; *(bottom)* © Ken Ross/FPG International
18 © 1993 Kenton/Zefa/H. Armstrong Roberts
35 *(all)* © 1994 Erika Stone
41 *(left to right)* © Daniel Bosler/Tony Stone Worldwide; courtesy United Airlines; K. Carpenter/H. Armstrong Roberts
43 *(left to right)* E. Alan McGee/FPG International; SuperStock; © 1994 Erika Stone; SuperStock
44 *(top)* J. B. Grant/Leo de Wys Inc.; *(bottom)* © J. Barry O'Rourke/The Stock Market
47 *(left)* © 1993 Dick Luria/FPG International; *(middle and right)* © 1994 Erika Stone
52 *(top)* © Daniel Bosler/Tony Stone Worldwide; *(middle)* Leo de Wys Inc./Leo de Wys; *(bottom)* © 1989 Chris Mihulka/The Stock Market
53 *(top, left to right)* Camerique/H. Armstrong Roberts; M. Elenz-Tranter/H. Armstrong Roberts; SuperStock; © Keith Olson/Tony Stone Worldwide; *(bottom, left to right)* ©1987 Jon Feingersh/The Stock Market; © 1992 T. Tracy/FPG International; SuperStock
57 ©1991 Mark Harmel/FPG International
58 and **59** Noreen O'Connor-Abel
65 *(top row, left to right)* © Jeffrey W. Myers/The Stock Market; SuperStock; © 1991 Mike Valeri/FPG International; © Kevin Michael Daly/The Stock Market; *(second row, left to right)* © Steve Brown, Sporting Pictures (UK) Ltd/Leo de Wys, Inc.; © Anne-Marie Weber/The Stock Market; © Stephen Simpson/FPG International
66 *(top to bottom)* Noreen O'Connor-Abel; Noreen O'Connor-Abel; Howard G. Ross/FPG International; © Ken Straiton/The Stock Market
67 *(left to right)* © T. Quing/FPG International; © Lee Kuhn/FPG International; © 1990 A. Schmidecker/FPG International
73 *(clockwise from left)* SuperStock; David Young Wolff/PhotoEdit; © Harvey Lloyd/The Stock Market; © Bill Wassman/The Stock Market
75 *(ear)* Tif Hunter/Tony Stone Images; *(all others)* © 1994 Erika Stone

79 Photograph by Brian Douglas. From *Having Our Say*, by Sarah and A. Elizabeth Delany with Amy Hill Hearth. Published by Kodansha America Inc. © Amy Hill Hearth, Sarah Louise Delany, and Annie Elizabeth Delany.
82 FPG International; © 1992 Richard Laird/FPG International; © R. Lord/The Image Works; © Jose Luis Banus – March 1991/FPG International; Jeffrey Sylvester/FPG International; Jon Levy/Liaison; Research Photogs/FPG International; © 1991 John Medere/The Stock Market
87 *(clockwise from top left)* © 1988 Naoki Okamato/ The Stock Market; © 1991 Vladimir Pcholkin/FPG International; © Dan Lecca/FPG International; Noreen O'Connor-Abel
93 *(clockwise from top left)* Archive Photos; The Bettmann Archive; Archive Photos/Camerique; H. Armstrong Roberts
94 *(left to right)* Historical Pictures Service, Chicago; UPI/Bettmann; Georges De Keerle © Gamma Liaison
95 *(left to right)* Reuters/Bettmann; UPI/Bettmann Newsphotos; © 1992 Warner Bros./SuperStock

99 *(clockwise from top left)* Gamma Liaison; © Holmes-Lebel 1932/FPG International; Archive Photos/Lambert; SuperStock
105 *(clockwise from top left)* J. S. Dorl/Pure Bred Dogs/*American Kennel Gazette*; Reuters/Bettmann; © Richard Danoff/The Stock Market
IC–2 SuperStock
IC–4 SuperStock
IC–7 *Pyramids, Great Wall, and Taj Mahal:* SuperStock; *Acropolis:* Leo de Wys Inc./J. B. Grant
IC–12 © 1992 Jon Feingersh/The Stock Market
IC–15 *(clockwise from top left)* © Daemmrich/Stock Boston; © 1992 Jon Feingersh/The Stock Market; © 1991 Michael Krasowitz/FPG International; Mark Lewis/Tony Stone Images
IC–17 *(clockwise from top left)* Stephen McBrady/ PhotoEdit; © 1993 Ariel Skelly/The Stock Market; © 1991 Lawrence Migdale/Stock Boston; © Edward Lettau/FPG International
IC–20 *(clockwise from top left)* Robert W. Young/ FPG International; © Paul Barton/The Stock Market; © Roy Morsch/The Stock Market; © Paul Barton/The Stock Market

Author's Acknowledgments

A great number of people assisted in writing *Interchange Intro*. Particular thanks go to the following:

The **students** and **teachers** in the following schools and institutes who pilot tested components of *Interchange Intro*; their valuable comments and suggestions helped shape the content of the entire course:

Adult ESL Resource Centre, Toronto, Canada; **The Bickford Centre,** Toronto, Canada; **Centro Cultural Salvadreño,** El Salvador; **Centro Internacional de Idiomas Maestros Asociados, S.C.,** Mexico; **Connections Language Consultants, Inc.,** Edmonton, Canada; **Dorset College,** Vancouver, Canada; **English Academy,** Japan; **Eurocentres,** Alexandria, Virginia, U.S.A.; **Fairmont State University,** West Virginia, U.S.A.; **Truman College,** Chicago, Illinois, U.S.A.; **Instituto Cultural de Idiomas Ltda,** Brazil; **Instituto Mexicano-Norteamericano de Cultura,** Mexico; **Language Resources,** Kobe, Japan; **Nippon Information and Communication Co.,** Japan; **Tokushima Bunri University,** Japan; and **University of California at Los Angeles Extension,** California, U.S.A.

And **editors** and **advisors** at Cambridge University Press, who provided guidance during the complex process of writing classroom materials:

Suzette André, Colin Bethell, Sarah Coleman, Riitta da Costa, Steve Dawson, Peter Donovan, Sandra Graham, Colin Hayes, John Haywood, Steven Maginn, Jane Mairs, Carine Mitchell, Noreen O'Connor-Abel, Susan Ryan, Helen Sandiford, Chuck Sandy, Ellen Shaw, Koen Van Landeghem, and Mary Vaughn.